CIDEROLOGY

Inspired by Joyce and Jean

An Hachette UK Company
www.hachette.co.uk

First published in Great Britain in 2018 by
Spruce, a division of Octopus Publishing Group Ltd
Carmelite House
50 Victoria Embankment
London EC4Y 0DZ
www.octopusbooks.co.uk
www.octopusbooksusa.com

Design and Layout Copyright © Octopus Publishing Group 2018
Text Copyright © Gabriel Cook 2018

Distributed in the US by
Hachette Book Group
1290 Avenue of the Americas
4th and 5th Floors
New York, NY 10104

Distributed in Canada by
Canadian Manda Group
664 Annette St.
Toronto, Ontario, Canada M6S 2C8

ISBN 978-1-84601-565-6

A CIP catalogue record for this book is available from the British
Library.

Printed and bound in China

10 9 8 7 6 5 4 3 2 1

Consultant Publisher: Sarah Ford
Assistant Editor: Ellie Corbett
Copy Editor: Caroline Taggart
Art Director: Juliette Norsworthy
Designer: Geoff Fennell
Illustrator: Agnese Bicocchi
Picture Research Manager: Giulia Hetherington
Senior Production Manager: Peter Hunt

CIDEROLOGY

FROM HISTORY AND HERITAGE TO THE CRAFT CIDER REVOLUTION

GABE COOK

spruce

CONTENTS

INTRODUCTION

My name is Gabe and I am The Ciderologist. I am passionate about cider and perry and rather magnificently I have become one of those lucky people who has turned a passion into a profession.

My story starts in a bucolic corner of England, not too far from Wales, in the county of Gloucestershire. This area is unspeakably pretty and is emblematic of classic, soft, intimate English countryside. This is an interwoven fabric of rolling hills, old orchards, grazing meadows, streams, woodlands and copses.

It is this place that I refer to as The Shire. Maybe I call it this because it exudes a Hobbiton-esque beauty and rustic nature? Or maybe it's because the people of this area are rather short and have unnaturally hairy feet? The Shire is not a defined area; it's not rooted in modern geopolitical boundaries. It's a landscape, a heritage, a culture; where old customs and a slower pace of life can still be found.

I was privileged, therefore, to have grown up in the village of Dymock, a settlement of pre-Roman origin, right in the heart of The Shire. Dymock is most famous for the vivid yellow carpet of wild daffodils that is rolled out by Mother Nature in the woodlands, uncultivated meadows and hedgerows surrounding the village every March. This scene is most memorably captured by the famous American poet Robert Frost – who lived in the village for a time – in his poem "The Road Not Taken".

The village of Dymock has a long-standing heritage of orchards, cider and perry. It is the only village in the UK (or maybe the world? Come on, someone prove me wrong!) to have an eponymous cider apple, perry pear and plum variety.

My love of nature and landscape, combined with some high-level map reading and colouring-in skills, led to a geography degree at the University of Leeds. Returning back to The Shire one summer I went to see what a "proper" cider farm looked like and so I visited Broome Farm, home of the Ross-on-Wye Cider & Perry Company, and met legendary cider maker (and now dear friend), Mike Johnson. I emerged from the cellar some two hours later with one large grin, two rosy cheeks, three voluptuous cider cakes and nine bottles of perry and cider (as well as an elder brother to drive me home – drink responsibly folks!).

OPPOSITE: Gabe in his happy place.

The Shire: it's a landscape, a heritage, a culture, where old customs and a slower pace of life can still be found.

Some years later after graduating, working in a dead-end job and undertaking my first lap of the planet, I went back to Broome Farm, where I was promptly offered the opportunity to help Mike make cider. The role even came with accommodation. It was billed as a "timbered chalet among myriad fruit trees". In reality it was a shed in the garden. But as a 23-year-old, who had spent the whole of the year living out of a sleeping bag that smelled like the inside of a packet of dry-roasted peanuts, The Shed was bloody perfect.

It was a privilege to work for Mike, learning by his side the skill of the process, the knowledge of the fruit and the subtlety of the blending. Of greatest significance, Mike encouraged me to make a perry from the last tree on Granny Joyce's farm in Dymock. I know that my Grandad Bill – who died before

ABOVE: The idyllic village of Dymock, in Gloucestershire – a place of wild daffodils, timeless poets and someone who talks about cider for a living.

I was born – had picked fruit from this tree, and so had generations before him.

While grubbing around on the floor, picking up these pears, I had an epiphany that would change everything. I could see so very clearly how cider and perry was at the crux of everything I was passionate about: local history, wildlife, culture, traditions and ancestry. An incredible sense of place and connection to my landscape and my forebears flowed over me. I had found my calling. I knew that cider and perry was the path for me.

A year later, Westons Cider, the UK's fifth-biggest producer, and handily located in the nextdoor village of Much Marcle, kindly knocked on the door and offered me the opportunity to be their Assistant Cider Maker. So, I went from making cider in 200-litre (53-gallon) oak barrels to 200,000-litre (53,000-gallon) stainless steel tanks. Gulp.

However, after two years on a steep, but immensely satisfying, learning curve, I had come to realize that I gained more satisfaction from, and was probably better at, talking about cider than making it.

So when H P Bulmer Ltd, the world's largest cider maker, based in Hereford, England, asked if I would like to be their Cider Communications Manager, I jumped at the chance. Yes, I got paid for talking about cider, and I did so, very happily, for three years.

The highlight of my tenure in this role had to be when I had the opportunity to present a bottle of cider to Queen Elizabeth II as part of her Diamond Jubilee tour in 2012. The moment passed in the blink of an eye, but I do seem to remember Liz being a little bemused/perplexed/frightened by the whole experience.

I then took a slightly different tack. Having travelled there in 2006, New Zealand held a fascination for me (amazing geography), and I had a long-standing ambition to live and work there. So I decided to apply for a visa and, bugger me, they let me in! Two years of subsequent cider making and wine making was not only a fabulous learning experience but also the facilitator to a wonderful way of life and the source of many a rip-roaring anecdote.

But, once again, like an unremitting siren, The Shire sang out to me and I returned back to its cidery bosom. When I was offered the chance to talk about cider for the biggest voice of all – the National Association of Cider Makers – it was too good an opportunity to turn down.

But in my heart I knew the path to cider nirvana. I needed to strike out on my own, and so The Ciderologist was born. It is my place, my voice, my *raison d'être* – a way to champion and advocate this great drink and great tradition by shouting about it from the rooftops.

People often to say to me, "What's your hobby?" Ideally, I'd like to respond by saying that I'm the bass clarinetist in a particularly funky acid jazz ensemble, or that I'm an origami master. But that would be fantasy. The fact is, for me, cider is all-consuming. It's my hobby, my job, my passion. And it's great. I wouldn't change a ruddy thing.

BELOW: The Shire in all its glory.

AN INTRODUCTION TO CIDEROLOGY

What is cider? In fairly dry terms, cider can be defined as the result of the fermentation of apple juice, whereby yeast converts sugar into alcohol. Although technically accurate, this definition barely scratches the surface of what cider is all about.

Search England through, search wider.
You'll never find a drink so kind as cider.

ANON

As you will come to discover, dear reader, cider is a bit of a chameleon. To its advantage, it covers a vast spectrum, ensuring that there is invariably the ideal cider for every person, on every occasion. However, this lack of singular identity can also be a disadvantage: there is no one thing for cider to hang its hat on. For me, however, it's quite simple. I believe that cider is the perfect confluence of art, science and nature.

ART Cider making is a creative process, and as with anything creative there is the opportunity for artistic expression, flair and originality. The majority of ciders are made with blends of different apples, and the intimate knowledge a cider maker has of the manifold varieties lets them paint a new canvas every year, thanks to the vagaries and nuances of each vintage.

SCIENCE As with any fermentation, there are scientific processes, steps and rules that need to be understood (or at least respected) in order to create a superior product. There are many Master of Brewing and Wine Science qualifications that are available

globally to ensure that such rigour can be applied throughout those industries.

There is less education specifically targeted toward the cider industry, with just one or two individuals providing sound technical training. However, with cider's global popularity on the rise, this shortage of higher-education-standard training will be remedied.

NATURE We rely on wildlife to achieve the whole process of cider making, through the work of yeast and bacteria. Of course, modern cider makers use cultured yeasts that have been carefully bred and selected over years or decades. Bold and powerful, they are the Belgian Blue cows of the microflora world.

But, for any cider maker undertaking a wild fermentation, natural yeast and bacteria play an incredibly important role. They determine a large proportion of the flavour and aromatic profile. Encouraging, and working with, helpful wildlife is crucial – treat them with respect and they will work for you.

Of course, nature is also prevalent in the orchard – it is an environment alive with wildlife. Predators abound here, whether they be invertebrates such as earwigs and ladybirds or insect-munching birds.

THE CIDER ISSUE

It isn't always easy to get people engaged with cider. I get a somewhat quizzical look when I tell folk that I am a (self-appointed) cider expert. Fine-wine expertise is highly regarded and lauded – a noble profession. To be a beer aficionado is to be a facial hair-adorned millennial with a finger on the pulse of all that is cool, craft and contemporary. Whisk(e)y masters live in an eternal state of elegance, wearing velvet smoking jackets and lounging in wingback chairs.

Alas, such positivity is not often afforded to the humble fermented apple. It's almost certain that if anyone were to undertake a straw poll on the street, and asked everyone the question, **"WHAT DOES CIDER MEAN TO YOU?"**, they would be given one of the following three responses:

1. **I DRANK 6 PINTS OF SUPER MEGA BLEND WHEN I WAS 14 AND HAD THE WORST HANGOVER IN THE HISTORY OF THE UNIVERSE.**

I DON'T DRINK IT.

2. **IT'S WHAT THE PARK-BENCH ORATOR IS DRINKING AT 8.35 EVERY MORNING AS I WALK TO WORK.**

I DON'T DRINK IT.

3. **ROUGH SCRUMPY! DAD DRANK 4 PINTS WHEN WE WERE ON HOLIDAY IN DEVON WHEN I WAS A CHILD, AND HIS LEGS DIDN'T WORK PROPERLY, SO HE FELL IN A DITCH. IT WAS HILARIOUS. BUT IT WAS RANK STUFF.**

I DON'T DRINK IT.

The reality is that these are common preconceptions among a large proportion of the population in the UK, and possibly elsewhere in the world, and understandably so because they are all real experiences. But it doesn't have to be this way.

Cider and perry can be the finest drinks in the land. They can have as much class and finesse as any wine, and as much attitude and boldness as craft beer. The issue is that the majority of those involved in the wider drinks industry, never mind the consumers, are unaware of this potential.

I have therefore taken it upon myself to utilize my decade-plus of knowledge, passion and loudness to let the world become aware of the opportunity that cider and perry provide. I call it Ciderology.

There's no denying it: the terms Ciderologist and Ciderology are made up. The words are a touch silly. But there's also method in my madness. They're obviously connected with cider, and an "ology" is a subject of study, or a branch of knowledge. Suddenly it seems to make sense, right?

Ciderology is an ethos; a way of life, if you will. You could call me a cider Jedi. But please don't. As The Ciderologist, I have embarked upon a journey to spread the good word of cider and perry.

Q. WHAT IS CIDEROLOGY?

CIDEROLOGY

{saɪ.də'ɒlə.dʒi}

Noun

A. **1.** THAT WHICH IS PRACTISED BY THE CIDEROLOGIST

2. THE STUDY, TEACHING AND CHAMPIONING OF CIDER

THE PRINCIPLES OF
CIDEROLOGY
ARE UPHELD BY SIX CORE VALUES

1.

HAVE A TRUE LOVE OF CIDER AND PERRY: THE PERFECT CONFLUENCE OF ART, SCIENCE AND NATURE.

2.

ESPOUSE THE UNIQUE TRADITIONS, HERITAGE, CULTURE AND IDENTITY OF CIDER IN ITS HEARTLAND REGIONS.

3.

ADVOCATE THE DEVELOPMENT OF SUSTAINABLE, AUTHENTIC CIDER INDUSTRIES IN AREAS OF NEW GROWTH.

4.

CHAMPION PRODUCERS FOR THEIR INNOVATION AND CREATION OF PRODUCTS WITH HIGH VALUE PERCEPTION (HVP).

5.

SUPPORT CIDER PRODUCERS OF ALL SCALES WHO UPHOLD THE SPIRIT OF CIDER BY MAKING A RESPONSIBLE PRODUCT AND CONTRIBUTING TO THEIR LOCAL HERITAGE, ECONOMY, ENVIRONMENT AND COMMUNITY.

6.

CELEBRATE AND SHARE THE WONDER OF CIDER WITH THE WORLD.

GLOBAL OUTLOOK

This book, and Ciderology as a whole, have a global perspective. Before I left the UK for New Zealand I very much had a thinking that English West Country cider apples were all that could be used to make an interesting and high-value product, and that dessert apples were a bit rubbish. What a naïve twerp. That's like saying that a Sauvignon Blanc is inferior to a Malbec because it's not quite so big, bold or tannic. No! They're just different. One can only make a judgment call about the cider in question upon tasting it and deciding whether the cider is a) well made and b) made in a style to one's personal palate preference.

Thankfully, after producing and consuming cider and perry of all styles in New Zealand,

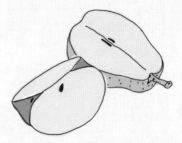

and now around the world, made with a plethora of dessert apples and other fruits, I have engaged global cidervision. It's all about context – time, place, who you're with, whether you're eating food, whether you are after the most fancy-pants things on the drinks list. The great thing is that cider and perry can be the right decision in all these situations.

But Ciderology is far more than simply the production of an alcoholic beverage. In certain parts of the world cider forms an integral part of the culture, heritage, lifeblood; it may even be *the* defining feature. It can be imbued with rich history, countless fables, Shakespearean-esque characters, fun, laughter and an inexorable connection to the land. It can also be modern, urban, contemporary, bonkers and experimental.

Ultimately, Ciderology is an excuse for me not actually to live in the real world, because, you know, talking about cider isn't a real job, is it? Well, apparently, it can be. I like to think I've taken the advice of famed cider fan Confucius. He said, "Choose a job you love and you will never have to work a day in your life." I have decided to follow this path.

Mind you, Confucius also said, "Never give a sword to a man who can't dance", so what did he know?

BELOW: The West of England has a proud cider heritage, but it is only one chapter of the global cider story.

THE STATE
OF CIDER

There is no doubt about it. Globally, cider and perry are in a more exciting place, and with greater potential for true recognition and understanding by a wide audience, than ever before. There is renewed interest in the "old world" countries of established tradition, such as France and Spain. Others, such as Luxembourg and Switzerland, where the old customs of cider making disappeared in the 20th-century drive for agricultural industrialization, are just waking up to their heritage once again.

But it is from the "new world" – areas without a pre-existing, or essentially lost, cider heritage – that this global cider renaissance is being driven. The likes of the USA, New Zealand and Australia are nations of pioneering, entrepreneurial spirit, quality apple-producers and makers of fine beverages. The stage has been set and the players are now treading the boards with aplomb.

So what sparked this spotlight on cider? To answer this, we must go back to the mother ship – the UK.

The time is the 1990s. The value perception of cider is at an all-time low. H P Bulmer Ltd's ill-fated plans for global expansion fail and it fell into administration, being bought by Scottish & Newcastle breweries in 2003. Taunton Cider has already long been bought and sold several times to large multinationals.

Cider's much maligned status through the latter part of the 20th century signals the challenges facing cider makers at the turn of the millennium.

RIGHT: The "new world" cider nations, and new thinking, are driving the global cider boom.

The "Magners effect": suddenly cider is the most sought-after drink on the market.

THE "MAGNERS" EFFECT

But, like the phoenix from the flames, British cider resurrects itself once again. This time, it's thanks to an unlikely source – an Irish producer. H P Bulmer bought a 50 percent stake in William Magners of Clonmel in 1937, and finalized the purchase nine years later. However, this ownership didn't last long and Bulmer sold the company in the 1950s, along with the rights to the Bulmer name in the Republic of Ireland.

Fast-forward 50 years, and this little Irish cider company has been acquired by C&C Group. Their main brand is known as Bulmers in the Republic of Ireland, but can't be called this elsewhere owing to the original agreement with H P Bulmer of Hereford. So, in 2006, this brand is launched into the UK under a new guise: Magners.

The timing is perfect: it is the hottest summer on record and coincides with the football World Cup – people are looking for a thirst-quencher in the pub garden. In comes Magners with a marketing campaign of about £30 million, centred around the unisex and social nature of their drink and, most crucially, that it should be drunk over ice.

Magners quickly becomes the liquid soundtrack to the summer. Most cleverly, the "over ice" serving not only keeps the cider cool, but as it is initially available only in a pint bottle, it requires the owner of the pint to take the bottle with them to the table. The ritual of the over-ice pour and the displaying of the badge to fellow drinkers are key factors in the brand's rapid success.

The response from competitors is immediate. A number of over-ice replicas come from other cider makers to form a new "premium category". Far removed from the white ciders and mainstream offering, this is a trendy drink, appealing to a younger demographic that doesn't have the emotional baggage of previous bad experiences with drinking cider.

All sizes and scale of cider maker benefit from this "Magners effect": from big producers to independents to little farmhouse operations. Suddenly cider is the most sought-after drink on the market. Supermarkets give cider multiple bays, which is unprecedented, and pubs have two or three ciders on draught. Small producers are frequenting farmers' markets and selling more from the farm gate. By 2009, UK volume has grown 50 percent from the 2006 figure. The cider renaissance has arrived.

GLOBAL GROWTH AND FLAVOURED CIDER

So where is cider right now? Stats from Global Data show that in the years 2011–16, global cider volumes increased by 4.8 percent. Cider is the world's second-fastest growing drinks category, sitting behind only spirits, which are up there because of the inflationary impact of the Indian and Chinese markets' proclivity for whisky.

This volume growth has come predominantly from the big brewers. In the global "mature" markets of Western Europe and North America, beer volumes had been in decline for some time, and big brewers eyed up the quick sales gains being achieved by cider in the UK. Since then, cider has begun to be presented not only in these markets, but in those of the "emerging" areas also – Australasia, Asia, Central and South America and Eastern Europe.

A considerable portion of this growth has been driven by a relatively new sector in the category – flavoured cider.

Adding fruits, herbs and spices to cider isn't new. There is plenty of reference in old texts to mustard being added to dodgy cider, to ginger being added to cider to make it a bit bolder, and to soft fruits being added so that it becomes more appealing to a female palate.

But fruit cider, as a drink of note, has been an important player only in the last 20 years or so. It has come to prominence largely thanks to the entrepreneurial spirit of some Scandinavian cider makers.

The 1990s saw a development of a category of drinks called RTDs (Ready To Drink). In the UK they were known as alcopops on account of their popularity among the 18–24 demographic. Generally made with a spirit base, and with added flavours, colours and sweeteners, these drinks became incredibly popular among their target audience.

OPPOSITE: The launch of this brand in 2006, and the over-ice proposition, spawned the "Magners effect" still being felt today.

BELOW: In the UK, the "Magners effect" helped small producers grow, and new cider makers come to market.

They also quite quickly caught the ire of the UK government because of their overt targeting of younger consumers. Legislation brought in in 1996 increased duty on them by 40 percent and alcopops gradually fell back into obscurity.

SCANDINAVIAN FRUIT CIDER

A decade later, a few Scandinavian cider makers, with one eye on the vacant RTD sector and the other on the new wave of consumers post "Magners effect", pushed hard with their brands into the UK. The combination of soft fruitiness, teeth-furringly high levels of sweetness and the new vogue for "cider" started to draw in the younger elements of the market.

Fruit cider, as a drink of note, has been an important player only in the last 20 years or so.

But here's my issue with some of the uber-commercial fruit ciders – there is little apple juice in them, and what little there is cannot be tasted. To my mind, cider in this context is just a vehicle for alcohol and sugar and these drinks are, all but in name, the new alcopops.

It is hard to believe that they represent the best of cider, and I believe that they might even act to obscure the wide range of ciders that are available today. You could argue that they act as "gateway" ciders: consumers try a fruit-flavoured cider and then go on a voyage of exploration through the broader cider category. But all the evidence suggests that this is not the case, especially in the UK, but also in Australia and Eastern Europe, where fruit ciders occupy large volumes.

I'm a fan of cleverly crafted flavoured ciders that exude balance and creativity. When made with skill, passion and quality raw materials, flavoured cider can pique the interests of inquisitive consumers and

MAJOR GLOBAL TRENDS

CIDER TYPES, 2016
DATA FROM GLOBAL DATA 2017

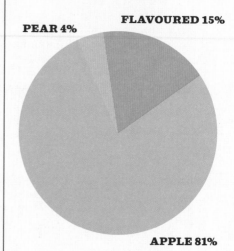

PEAR 4% FLAVOURED 15%

APPLE 81%

GROWTH BY CIDER TYPE, 2011–16
DATA FROM GLOBAL DATA 2017

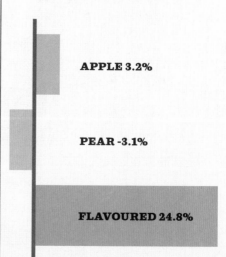

APPLE 3.2%

PEAR -3.1%

FLAVOURED 24.8%

get them engaged with the broader cider category, especially in the newer markets. Alas, I just don't think this is true of a lot of the mass-produced fruity styles. Consumers around the world are craving new, innovative and different drinks. But they deserve to have something made with quality and care, not sugar and artificial aroma.

THE CRAFT REVOLUTION

Despite global cider volumes being on the increase, if we break down the numbers, it makes for interesting reading. In the UK, for the last five years plus, cider volumes have remained stagnant, with the huge popularity for flavoured ciders plugging the gap created by consumers turning their back on mainstream, commercial, mildly tannic ciders. In the USA, after a few short years of rapid growth, 2016 saw a total decrease in cider volumes.

You could take these figures and bemoan the end of the cider boom. But, if you dig a little deeper under the numbers, you can see a different trend emerging. In the UK, volumes of what are known as craft and heritage brands by the broader category have seen a volume increase of about 10 percent, while in the USA the value of regional brands continues to grow and thrive.

It's all about the statistics, you see. It's reminiscent of that great quote from Andrew Lang, Scottish folklorist and novelist, who once said, "He uses statistics as a drunken man uses a lamppost – for support rather than illumination."

So, what's going on? What we're talking about here is the Craft Revolution.

Anyone who isn't aware of what craft beer is must surely have been living under a rock for the last few years. Well, that's a slightly disingenuous remark, given that craft beer has no clear definition from any

legal or technical point of view. It's all about attitude and personality. And hops. Lots of big, fat, intensely aromatic and bittering hops. Apart from when it's not like that at all, as with coffee porters or New England IPAs. It's complicated. Go check out one of the really good books on the subject.

What is certain is that at their heart, these drinks are bold and packed full of quality materials. Most crucially, the term "craft" applies to the brewery as well as the beer – a craft brewer makes craft beer. And what makes a craft brewer? Well, again, there is no legal definition, but it generally boils down to being small(er), independent and sticking it to the man. Which is great, right up until the point at which the brewery is sold to one of the big boys, and ceases to be craft overnight. It's a tough world.

So, who's drinking craft beer? In the UK, the lazy (but sometimes accurate) stereotype fits into the "hipster" model: beard (check), lumberjack shirt (check), tattoos (check), skinny jeans (check). Denizens of once grotty areas of major cities all over the world, these millennials have money to burn and they choose to burn it on beer that is packed full of flavour, is presented in innovative packaging (such as 330ml/12oz cans) and has intelligent branding.

Actually, craft beer is being drunk by anybody who wants to try something different, to drink something flavoursome and to have a great experience. It's not about how much you can drink, it's about how much you can enjoy the drink. Some people balk at the fact that the serving size tends to be smaller for these styles of beers, but the whole point is experimentation, and when a

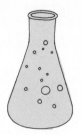

Double IPA comes in at 9 percent ABV, who wants to be chugging back a pint anyhow?

What craft does, though, is create a High Value Perception (HVP). People are willing to pay more for such items – they know they're more expensive to make (because the scale of economies has worked against the smaller producer) and they genuinely believe that they are getting value for money (because what they're buying tastes great).

What we're talking about here is the craft revolution.

This "craft" attitude has transcended beer. Craft gin has exploded – in 2011–12 there were five distillery licence applications in the UK, whereas in 2014–15 there were a mother-ruining 65! The concept of craft permeates so much of food and drink culture today. And a marvellous thing it is, too: artisanal bread, urban mead, chorizo – *even* Parmesan biscotti. The range of skilfully created products is greater than ever before and is something to be digested with joy.

TO CRAFT OR NOT TO CRAFT?

Undoubtedly the craze for craft has permeated into cider and has driven an interest in smaller, regional and heritage ciders across the globe. Entirely expectedly and understandably, a great many of these producers position themselves as being craft cider makers producing craft ciders.

OPPOSITE: Cider can exude as much cool, contemporary, youthful character as any craft beer.

The quandary to ponder is whether these producers should be utilizing the "craft" tag. Given that almost anything that isn't rampantly mainstream and commercial is considered a craft product these days, has the term lost its value? Have we entered the post-craft world?

In the UK, craft cider has different connotations and uses. There are a band who define craft cider as being as it was in their grandfather's day: *the juice, the whole juice and nothing but the juice*. Their focus is on celebrating heritage, through the use of traditional, high-tannin, West Country apples and minimal intervention; and heaven forbid adding anything else to it.

For others craft cider is the complete opposite. It means innovation, contemporary thinking and creativity without boundaries. Hops, elderflowers, fruits and spices, among myriad other ingredients, are being used to create a whole new world of cider styles and flavours. Very often these producers are outside the classic West Country cider heartland, with strong influence from the beer category.

For some larger producers, the mere act of putting a cider in a 330-ml (12-oz) can is sufficient to proclaim it a craft product. It is a point of contention as to whether one is a craft cider *maker* or whether one can simply create a craft *cider*. Discuss...

> *Undoubtedly the craze for craft has permeated into cider and has driven an interest in smaller, regional and heritage ciders across the globe.*

But if not craft, then what other term can these producers use to distinguish themselves from the run of the mill? A few different labels have emerged:

- **FINE** Exuding wine-like qualities, with finesse and elegance.

- **WILD/NATURAL** Wild yeast fermented, with an emphasis on varietals and *terroir*.

- **ORCHARD** The focus being on orchards, varietals and *terroir*.

- **MODERN** Contemporary, sleek.

- **PROGRESSIVE** Boundary-pushing, edgy.

As is so often the case, there is no simple answer. The best drinks tend to incorporate elements of different trains of thought, trying to capture the best of everything. It's normally best to let the cider do the talking, so here is a simple five-point test that helps distinguish a cider worth celebrating. It needs to be:

- **MADE WITH SKILL** A cider can be as traditional as you like, made with love, care and unicorn's tears. But if it smells like the inside of a packet of dry-roasted peanuts or deserves to be spread over your fish and chips, then that's no good. There's nothing wrong with a bit of funk, but the James Brown factor needs to be in proportion to the other flavours and aromas.

ABOVE: Craft cider making of the urban persuasion, at Hawkes in London.

● **INTERESTING** A rubbish label, perhaps, but it'll have to do. It means the cider has to stand out from the crowd in some way and not just be another generic, medium-sweet, mildly tannic cider. This X factor could be achieved through the judicious and balanced addition of other flavours, or through smart, creative use of wild yeasts, oak vessels, arrested fermentation or any other number of factors.

● **AUTHENTIC** Made with heart and soul, with people, place and passion at its core. The cider needs to back up the story on the label and vice versa.

● **RECOMMENDABLE** It still needs to be enjoyable, something that you would gladly drink again and tell all your friends about. What's the point in making something so complex or "out there", or just so damn funky, that a punter wouldn't want to order another one?

● **OF A HIGH VALUE PERCEPTION (HVP)** Finally, and most importantly, a cider worth celebrating needs to showcase the best of what cider can be, and not the lowest common denominator. It must be endowed with such beauty and awesome taste that people will be willing to fork out more because they think the product is worth the extra spend.

LOOKING TO THE FUTURE

Craft or not, the crucial thing is *cider makers do not stand still*. Yes, the wonderful cider making traditions, rituals and customs of the old world must be upheld and transferred to the next generation. They are a crucial part of the cultural identity to the regions they come from; without them we become one big homogenous cultural blob. But at the same time cider needs to ensure that it remains innovative and relevant. And if that means the addition of something other than apple, then so be it. Ultimately the cider needs to look good and taste good, too.

The likes of Lord Scudamore, Sir Kenelm Digby and the Bulmer brothers, who we shall meet in the next chapter, strove hard to ensure that cider was always taken to the next level of quality and popular appeal, through science, technology, creativity, innovation and sheer hard work. They weren't looking to the past, they were looking to the future: and so should we.

RIGHT: Cider and perry that exude quality and finesse and all of the other cues associated with high value products like wine.

THE JOURNEY
OF CIDER

The story of the apple is an incredible one. It dates back thousands of years, spans thousands of miles and involves the ingenuity and knowledge of classical civilizations. To quote notable cider and perry maker James Marsden, it's also a story about poo. Allow me to elucidate...

Any apple enthusiast must long to visit the Tien Shan mountain range, the beginning of all things for apples: to stand among the myriads shapes, sizes and colours of apple must be akin to time-travelling.

There has been much research exploring the origins of our domesticated apple varieties, especially over the last 30 years, and no one has done more insightful work than Dr Barrie Juniper from Oxford University. His 2006 book, *The Story of the Apple*, written alongside David Mabberley, wonderfully details this lineage.

Apples are part of the Rosaceae family, distantly related to other fruits, such as blackberries and stone fruits, as well as hawthorn trees and roses. The apple genus – *Malus* – probably arose in southern China and gradually spread itself all across the temperate range of the northern hemisphere, west toward Europe, and east (via the Bering Strait landbridge) into North America. Way back then, its fruit would have been what we now term crab apples – the *wild* apples.

THE BEGINNINGS OF APPLES

Cultivated (eating, cooking, cider) apples – *Malus domestica* – bear little resemblance to these natives. In searching for a common ancestor, prevailing research points to a species called *Malus sieversii*, which can still be found today, lurking in the foothills of the Tien Shan mountain range in Central Asia.

It's here, in Kazakhstan and Kyrgyzstan, that the last remnants of wild apple forest can be found. These genetic melting pots are sadly under threat through deforestation and climate change, but eminent pomologists are doing their utmost to learn as much as possible about these unique environments.

These protective, rugged mountains and fertile, sheltered valleys would have provided the last refugia for many plants and animals during the most recent ice age, enduring for 100,000 years and ending some 10,000 years ago. (And you thought winters today could be a bit miserable!)

Any apple enthusiast must long to visit this area, the beginning of all things for apples, and for cider. The landscape is breathtakingly beautiful – Tien Shan translates as "celestial mountain range". To stand among the myriad shapes, sizes and colours of apple, not to mention their diverse range of flavour properties, must be akin to time-travelling

*If you attempt to replicate an apple
variety by planting the pip in the ground,
you are going to be mightily disappointed.*

back to the beginning of creation itself. All the cultivated apples grown in the world today owe their parentage to this woodland range, and that is a mind-blowing thought.

Despite all these apples, there is no evidence to suggest that cider was made in Central Asia. In these unforgiving environments, why go to laborious, energy-sapping lengths to extract juice from a hard fruit, which will turn the precious sugar into alcohol? No, these folks valued the life-giving sugar, and so preferred to preserve apples by drying them for consumption over a period of time.

APPLES AND BEARS

So how did *Malus sieversii*, tucked away in Central Asia, become the progenitor of a multi-billion-dollar global industry? Well,

this is where the poo comes in. You see, apples are quite tasty if you're a bear, and bears were eating apples in giant quantities, naturally spreading the seed as they moved about. As the ice started to retreat, the bears extended their patch and roamed west.

Humans followed suit, and trans-continental trade routes, notably the Silk Road, began to establish themselves, and apple pips continued to hitch a ride west – this time in the guts of hungry pack horses.

Undoubtedly, some of these apples would have displayed characteristics that made them more appealing than the bitter and acidic wild apples. And thus humans, with a quick lob of an apple core, got involved in this westward spread, too, eventually reaching the Fertile Crescent: Mesopotamia – the land of the two rivers – in modern Iraq.

ABOVE: The wild apple forests of the Tien Shan mountain range are a unique melting pot of apple genetics.

THE FIRST FARMERS

The great civilizations of this region were among the first farmers. A settled population, a fertile soil and a constant flow of people and knowledge meant that Mesopotamia was one of the regions at the heart of the origins of agriculture.

The challenge with apples is that if you attempt to replicate an apple variety by planting the pip in the ground, you are going to be mightily disappointed, because it is essentially guaranteed that an entirely different variety will sprout.

The Mesopotamians, some 4,000 years ago, were the first to crack the code and find an answer: grafting (*see* page 35). This ingenious method of genetic transfer was, and still remains, the most important tool in the domestication of apples and pears.

As the Greeks and Romans learned to identify specific apples and pears, they continued to use grafting as a way of selecting varieties for individual properties, and the technique began to spread throughout their respective empires. The age of orchards had begun. An early mention of these new landscapes is given in Homer's *Odyssey*, from about the 8th century BC, and it becomes more widespread in Roman times, with accounts from Columella in the 1st century BC and Varro in the 1st century AD of the storing and selling of different varieties of apples and pears.

It is now that we come across the first references to apples and fermented beverages. Thanks to various accounts, such as that of Pliny the Elder's *Naturalis Historia*, as well as pictorial evidence in the form of mosaics, we know that cider was being made in the Roman Empire from the 1st century AD. The Hebrew word *shekhar* and its Arabic equivalent *sikhar* denote alcoholic drinks. Through the subsequent Greek *sikera* and the Latin *sicera*, these are the source of our English word *cider*, as well as *cidre* in French and *sidra* in Spanish.

ROMANS AND BRITAIN

It is thought that cider did not become as prevalent as wine early on because the fruit is so tough. While grapes can be easily squeezed, extracting juice from apples

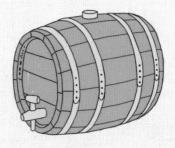

ABOVE: The Romans brought their horticultural skills and knowledge, along with their apples, into north-west Europe.

requires considerably more effort. So, it is with the advent of olive-mill technology, namely a stone mill and beam press, that it becomes possible to extract juice from apples more efficiently and thus to make cider. As the Roman Empire spread into northern Europe, so did their apples – what we know as dessert and cooking apples today.

There isn't much evidence to suggest that the Romans introduced cider making technology into Britain, but they certainly brought the concept of orcharding. It may be that the Romans arrived to find native Britons already making a "proto-cider" from crab apples.These small, wild, bitter apples would not have been edible, but we know that they were part of the diet of early Britons, because pips have been found near dwellings at archeological sites. The Greek historian Diodorus wrote in the 1st century BC of occasions when the Britons would become intoxicated by means of a fermented brew of honey or apples.

Some people think that the traditional, bold, tannic apples of northern France (and latterly of the West Country in England) are the result of the hybridization between the wild apples and the Roman-introduced cultivated apples. There's another school of thought, though, that suggests apples brought up from Spain were the progenitors of the high-tannin varieties of France and the UK today. This theory has some merit – there is evidence that cider was being made in northern Spain some 2,000 years ago.

CIDER POST-1066

Whatever their heritage, these apples, orchards and ultimately cider do not feature in British literature until well after the Norman Conquest of 1066. Proud Brits must take it on the chin that their apples are in fact French apples.

GRAFTING

The discovery of grafting was crucial to the selective breeding of apples and other fruits. Ensuring that identical genetic material is replicated is not straightforward, as those interested in apple-growing thousands of years ago discovered. Planting the pip of an apple in the ground would not result in the same variety growing. In order to produce fruit, pollen from another apple variety must fertilize the blossom. Although the fruit produced will be the same as the parent tree, the pips will be a cross between the two varieties. In addition to this, the vast majority of apples are not self-fertile – they cannot pollinate themselves and must rely on pollinating insects to transfer pollen. But, of course, there is no knowledge of which apple variety the pollinating insects have been visiting, further adding to the random genetic variation.

The answer to the conundrum of how to pass on genetic material was found in the process of grafting, whereby a spur of growing wood from the desired variety (known as scion wood) is taken and fixed onto a variety already planted that displays good rooting characteristics.

The tissues of the two elements combine, allowing water and nutrients to flow up into the graftwood, and the two varieties are bonded. This process is still the bedrock of the apple-growing industry today. When you look at any commercial apple trees, you're looking not at one variety, but two fused together.

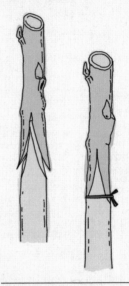

ABOVE: The "scion" wood is notched and secured onto a reciprocally cut rootstock, enabling the two to bond.

RIGHT: The union of the two apple varieties – the graft line – can be clearly seen on most apple trees.

ABOVE: Gardeners attending to their orchards in the 17th century. Apple-growing becomes more professional as subsistence farming declines.

The Domesday Book was an early census that the victorious Norman king, William the Conqueror, commissioned to assess his new English dominions, including the size of farms, population etc. There was little reference to apple orchards, but the Domesday Book did include reference to some 40-plus vineyards, mostly in the southern half of England, but also some in modern-day Yorkshire. Given that Leeds is not well known for claret these days, this would indicate something was climatically afoot.

The dates between 950 and 1250 are known as the Medieval Warm Period – the largest temperature spike of the last 7,000 years until the middle of the 20th century.

Attributed to solar activity and, my old favourite, thermohaline circulation (check it out – it's fascinating!), this meant that it wasn't until the period's end that apple-growing, and cider making, really starts to be referenced.

CIDER'S ZENITH

Market-gardening and fruit-growing expand in England during the 15th and 16th centuries, with a commercial attitude to agriculture, including orcharding and cider making, starting to supersede subsistence farming. But cider's zenith comes in the 17th century, thanks to political circumstances and a band of influential religious, scientific and aristocratic advocates. Henry Jeffreys, in his book, *Empire of Booze* (2016) wonderfully details the complex set of factors informing cider's growth during this period.

Picture the scene: Britain is almost permanently at war with its various European

and knowledge abounding, it would appear that cider was the craft beer of the 17th century! The age of cider had truly begun.

REDSTREAK

First among the influential figures is Lord Scudamore, ambassador to France from 1634 to 1639, who returned to his seat of Holme Lacy House in Herefordshire armed with a number of seedlings of unnamed French cider-apple varieties. He planted these up on his estate and one, subsequently named the Herefordshire Redstreak, was a resounding success. Such was the precocity of the tree – meaning that it produced fruit from a young age – and the quality of the juice that Evelyn noted it was by "the noble example

LEFT: The diarist and gardener John Evelyn, author of *Pomona* – the seminal text on cider from the 17th century.

neighbours – France, the Netherlands and Spain – often all at once. As well as putting a financial burden on the nation, this critically cuts off the supply of wine, which the British aristocracy have been consuming in great quantities. There is now an imperative to create an indigenous drink that could match wine's quality and appeal. And that drink, naturally, is cider.

At the forefront of this rallying cry for cider is the diarist and gardener John Evelyn. His treatise on cider, *Pomona*, published in 1664, is a detailed review on the merits and benefits of cider – the first of its kind. It also contained essays from other eminent cider experts of the age, talking with great authority on this most topical of subjects. With such heated passion

RIGHT: The Herefordshire Redstreak, in all its glory, beautifully presented in the *Pomona Herefordiensis* (1811).

of Lord Scudamore, and some more public-spirited gentlemen in those parts, that all Herefordshire is become, in a manner, an entire orchard."

The reputation of the fine ciders produced from this apple quickly spread – and lasted for decades.

FIRST BUBBLES

During the same period, the English courtier Sir Kenelm Digby was making an equally telling contribution. He established a glass furnace in the Forest of Dean in Gloucestershire to manufacture wine bottles which, through the use of coke instead of coal, the inclusion of an extra-long wind tunnel and a high ratio of minerals, created bottles that were stronger and more stable than any other in their day.

Their first use was not for wine, however, but for cider – and no ordinary cider at that. These strong containers enabled a final portion of fermentation to be completed within the bottle, ensuring that the cider was kept free from spoilage and, most importantly, adding a light, natural sparkle. What we are talking about is the *méthode traditionnelle*, aka the Champagne process. But Digby's experiments were being done before Benedictine monk and Champagne founding father Dom Perignon had even found his way from the monastery to the winery. We have legitimate cause, therefore, to describe this as being the "Forest of Dean" method rather than the "Champagne" method, but it's possible that the French wouldn't go for that!

Alas, this golden age of cider was not to last. It fell from grace and from the nobility's dinner table. As early as 1796 it was being reported that "the Redstreak Apple is given up". But why? Well, partly because the attention span, and brand loyalty, of monied imbibers in the 18th century was as short as that of a 21st century teenager. When other drinks, such as port, became available, cider was dropped from the nobility's table quicker than a losing lottery ticket. But the straw that broke the camel's back was entirely home made.

CIDER RIOTS!

The single greatest contributory factor of cider's fall from grace from flute-supping nectar to the agricultural worker's swill was the Cider Bill of 1763. This was a measure introduced by the government of Prime Minister Lord Bute to help reduce the National Debt, which had escalated wildly owing to

LEFT: For a time, cider (or cyder) was the drink of the elite, quaffed from beautiful, tall, crystal flutes.

Britain's involvement in the Seven Years' War. Central to the bill was the imposition of a tax of four shillings per hogshead of cider, enforceable by warrantless excise officers. Needless to say, this didn't go down too well in cider's West Country heartland.

The tax on cider prompted mournful processions, full rioting and the burning of effigies. In his opposition to this heresy, the Leader of the Whig Opposition, William Pitt "The Elder", stated:

> The poorest man may in his cottage bid defiance to all the forces of the Crown. It may be frail; its roof may shake; the wind may blow through it; the storm may enter; the rain may enter; but the King of England cannot enter – all his force dares not cross the threshold of the ruined tenement!

Interestingly enough, it is believed that this argument is the basis of the Fourth Amendment to the Constitution of the United States, that forbids unreasonable searches and seizures of individuals and property.

The government, in the face of impassioned pleas from the William Pitt "The Elder", backed down in 1766. The *Gloucester Journal* reported: "There is nothing heard in our streets, but 'the day of the oppressor is over, the calamity of the cyder drinker is put away; the deadly excise man shall appear no more in our quarters.'"Although the Cider Bill was repealed relatively quickly, it seems the damage had been done. In fact, the Cider Bill was probably the straw that broke the camel's back, with support for the

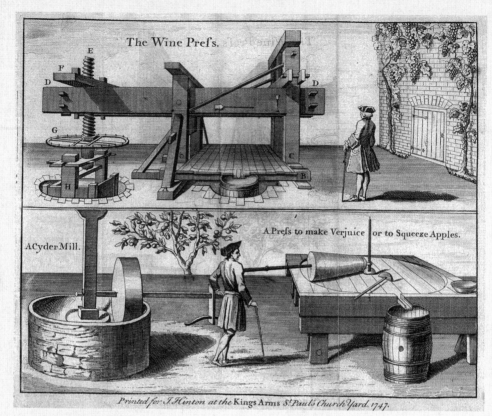

The Wine Press.

E
F
D
D
G
C
B
H

A Cyder Mill.

A Press to make Verjuice or to Squeeze Apples.

Printed for J. Hinton at the Kings Arms St. Pauls Church Yard. 1747.

ABOVE: Cider-making technology advances from the 18th century.

drink among the upper echelons already waning. Britain started warring less with Europe and drinking more port. This was much more to aristocratic English tastes, and as port's popularity soared, cider started its downward spiral into the domain of the agricultural classes, and in many ways has not reached those giddy heights since.

CIDER GOES INDUSTRIAL

During the 18th century a few cider making families – such as Gaymers in Norfolk, Aspalls in Suffolk and Symonds in Herefordshire –

had established themselves as prosperous concerns, but the greatest cider making dynasty had to wait another century.

So it is in the context of an increasingly urbanized and industrialized society that we approach the end of the 19th century. In the 1880s, Britain is in the midst of an agricultural depression, with landowners seeking new means of extracting value from the land.

It was a Herefordshire cider maker who grasped the nettle and revolutionized the way cider was made and consumed. Enter centre stage, H P Bulmer Ltd. The following improbable story of the foundation of this cider colossus is well documented in the pamphlet, *Early Days of Cider Making*, written by E F (Fred) Bulmer in 1937, on the occasion of the 50th anniversary of the founding of the company. H P Bulmer Ltd was founded in 1887 by H P (Percy) Bulmer in the village of Credenhill. Percy had been a sickly child, confined to bed with asthma for most of his schooldays. Although bright, he did not have the requisite education to go on to university, so he decided to start a business of his own. His father, the Reverend C H Bulmer, was passionate and knowledgeable on everything to do with the land and was a contributor to the *Herefordshire Pomona*, the great 19th-century catalogue of the pears and apples of the county. When Percy's mother suggested his business be something to do with eating or drinking because "these things never go out of fashion", he decided on cider making.

And so, in the autumn of 1887, Percy made his first 40 casks of cider, with the help of a millstone, press and Tommy the Pony – all courtesy of the farm next door. He quickly left Credenhill and established himself in the substantial market town of Hereford, first with a rental on Maylord Street and then settling on a plot of land on Ryelands Street.

Percy's brother, the aforementioned Fred Bulmer, joined him in 1889. A sharp, gregarious Cambridge graduate, Fred became the sales arm of the operation, but not before he had been offered the opportunity to tutor the children of the King of Siam. He declined, preferring to throw his lot in with Percy and have a crack at this cider making lark.

Thanks to the lure of cider, history was significantly altered. When Fred refused the King of Siam's offer, the role was instead filled by Anna Leonowens and spawned the novel *Anna and the King* and, of course, the Rodgers and Hammerstein musical *The King and I*. *Fred and the King* doesn't quite have the same ring, does it?

CIDER CHAMPAGNE

The brothers quickly understood that the key to making good cider was an understanding of the science behind the process. Such knowledge didn't really exist in the UK, but the French Champagne houses were masters of the control of fermentation. Fred and Percy decided that one of them needed to go over to France and learn.

The task fell to Percy who, during his bedridden, asthmatic youth, had taught himself French. In 1892–3, he spent three months with a Champagne firm in Epernay, and was given both the utmost in hospitality and the opportunity to learn about controlling the fermentation process.

On his return he brought this skill with him and the Bulmer brothers started to make their own Champagne cider – the finest

RIGHT: H P (Percy) Bulmer – founder of the eponymous cider company which went on to revolutionize cider making and remains the world's largest producer.

Britain had seen since the 17th century.

The firm's attention to scientific detail was further enhanced in 1905 through the recruitment of Dr Herbert Durham. A friend of Fred's from Cambridge, Herbert had specialized in tropical medicine and was part of a team of doctors who undertook research in some of the most deadly parts of the world. After ten years, the majority of the team were dead and Herbert himself was suffering from ill health.

The key to making good cider was an understanding of the science behind the process.

So after Herbert had paid a weekend visit to Hereford, Fred persuaded him that his skills as a scientist would be greatly appreciated. He promptly joined the company and worked there for the next 30 years. Under his leadership, the finest cider research facility was established, its crowning glory being the isolation of a yeast strain that was perfect for ensuring a clean cider. H P Bulmer use this yeast to this very day.

A LEGACY

H P Bulmer Ltd was quickly recognized as making the finest cider in the land. In 1911 it was awarded the Royal Warrant by King George V, and it still holds this notable title today. Percy Bulmer passed away in 1919 – his poor health taking him young. Fred carried on the business and continued its growth and expansion.

OPPOSITE: By the 1970s, cider makers such as Bulmers were forced in court by the powerful French wine region to drop the word "Champagne".

RIGHT: Alcohol advertising from a time when gender norms were rather more old-fashioned and entrenched!

APPLES:
AT THE CORE OF CIDER

OK, so here's a confession – I'm not much of a fan of apples. Well, what I mean to say is that I'm not much of a fan of eating apples. I remember when I was a little boy, the kindly local greengrocer would give me a beautiful, vivid green apple every time I went shopping with my Mum. And every time I'd nibble a little bit and then proclaim that I didn't like it. It obviously didn't scar me too much, however, for it is the celebration of the humble apple, in all its manifold forms, that is the basis of everything I do.

The variety of apple that is used to make a cider will go a long way in determining its aroma, flavour and mouthfeel.

Because here's the thing: the apple is (pardon the pun) at the core of all ciders. It should therefore come as no surprise that the variety of apple that is used to make a cider will go a long way in determining its aroma, flavour and mouthfeel. The obvious analogy, of course, is with wine, and rightly so, for cider in many ways is "temperate" wine.

Just as with grapes for wine, cultural and geographical factors have led to different types of apple being traditionally grown for making cider in different parts of Europe. In northern France, these were (and still are) characterized by the presence of tannins, and it is these apple varieties that William the Conqueror's descendants introduced into Britain. The West Country cider tradition was beginning.

Removed from their native environment and with new cultural influences and cross-breeding opportunities, a whole new raft of cider-apple varieties have developed in the UK over the last 700 years. This heritage of making cider from tannic apples was largely confined to the West of England, the good growing areas of the Southeast being given over to the production of fruit for the London table market.

But it wasn't until the 19th century that a truly scientific approach to cider-apple documentation began in the UK. One of the first to contribute to it was the future President of the Royal Horticultural Society Thomas Andrew Knight: inheriting three separate estates in Herefordshire, he used the 4,000 hectares (10,000 acres) of land at his disposal to undertake considerable horticultural research.

From a cider perspective, his *pièce de résistance* appeared in 1811. Entitled *Pomona Herefordiensis*, it was the first published account of native cider-apple varieties. It contained descriptions of the fruit, their growing habit and properties, as well as beautiful hand-coloured plates. This text was instrumental in shedding light on an industry that was in the doldrums at this time. So much

knowledge of these varieties had been lost that it was essential to have a benchmark to ascertain what was understood and what was missing.

By the end of the 19th century, cider was starting its move from agricultural labourer's drink to commercial product. Accompanying this paradigm shift came organizations that sought to bring full scientific rigour and knowledge to the burgeoning industry. Top of the list was the National Fruit and Cider Institute, founded in 1903 just south of Bristol. It came to be known as the Long Ashton Research Station (LARS) and later branched out into fruit research.

The first director of this facility was a man by the name of B T P Barker, who quickly sought to establish an order among the myriad names, types and styles of cider apple being grown in the West of England. He used the relative proportions of the two main flavour

WEST COUNTRY CIDER APPLE CATEGORIES

	ACIDITY (g/L of malic acid)	TANNIN (g/L of tannic acid)
SHARP	> 4.5	< 2
BITTERSHARP	> 4.5	> 2
BITTERSWEET	< 4.5	> 2
SWEET	< 4.5	< 2

and aroma building blocks in apples – acidity and tannin – to create a classification. The result of his efforts was the English Cider Apple Classification System, still used to this day.

Most cider apples grown in the UK today fall into the "bittersweet" category. The presence of tannin makes them quite different from eating and cooking apples. The vast majority of these apples are unpleasant to eat, very bitter and with mouth-bending astringency. But it is precisely these properties that provide structure and complexity to the resultant cider.

A LANGUAGE FOR CIDER

I am a huge advocate of speaking about cider in the same way as we do about wine, because they are made in such similar ways and because wine has achieved the High Value Perception (HVP) that I would love to see given to cider. The fact that cider apples have nuances and differences, just as wine grape varietals do, only seems to bolster this proposition. What am I talking about? I am talking about vintage characteristics.

WEST COUNTRY CIDER APPLE CHARACTERISTICS

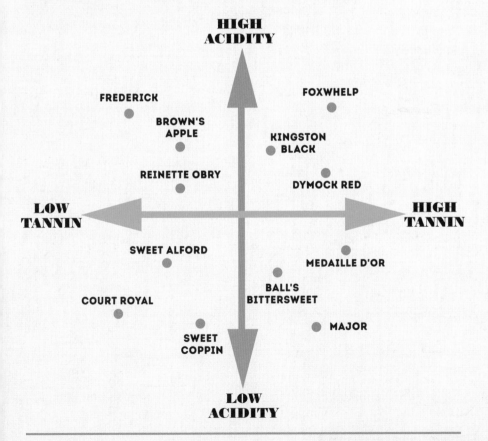

CIDER APPLES A–Z

There are literally hundreds of apple varieties grown all around the world to make cider, each with its own unique flavours and properties, and often with its own intriguing history. Here's a list of some of my favourites.

ASHTON BITTER – once lauded as a key early-season bittersweet, it's now known to produce a tree like a scarecrow, so has somewhat fallen out of favour.

BALL'S BITTERSWEET – sounds like a 1950s cough syrup and has the astringency to match. Developed by Percy Bulmer's nephew Edward Ball, the Bulmers pomologist in the 1920s.

CIDER LADY'S FINGER – not to be confused with something that lines the bottom of a tiramisu, Lady's Finger is thought to be a generic name to describe varieties that are long in shape, rather that broad, elliptical or round.

DABINETT – the most widely planted cider apple in Britain today owing to the quality of its juice and its fruiting precocity.

EGREMONT RUSSET – the definitive russet apple. Has the texture of psoriasis, but produces the most wonderfully lean, acidy and 'nutty' cider.

FOXWHELP – hails from the Forest of Dean in Gloucestershire and is one of the oldest recorded varieties, with its cider properties already well documented in 1664. The freshly milled apple pulp smells of strawberries and the fermented cider has a distinctive sherbet character.

GRAVENSTEIN – portmanteau apple name derived from famous English cricketer Tom Graveney and fictitious un-dead tinkerer Victor Frankenstein. Or not.

HARRY MASTERS JERSEY – named after a nurseryman from Woolston, Somerset. The term "Jersey" is used to describe apples of a decent astringency plus an idiosyncratic shape characterized by "broad shoulders" and a "narrow waist".

IMPROVED HANGDOWN – used to provide fruitiness in a blended cider and also as a haemorrhoids treatment.

JONAGOLD – A cross between Jonathan and Golden Delicious, it produces a soft and highly perfumed cider.

KINGSTON BLACK – the "king" of cider apples. End of.

LE BRET – named after the world's best basketball player, James Le Bret. Hang on...

MICHELIN – tastes like tyres.

NEWTOWN PIPPIN – US variety that became one of the first apples to be exported to the UK.

OVERLEAF – an extremely rare British variety, whose tree takes a weeping form. So much so that it has been described as looking like a dead octopus on a stick!

PIG'S NOSE – so named because its shape is reminiscent of...er...a pig's nose. (*And the Nobel Prize for Literature goes to Gabe Cook for his evocative description of cider-apple varieties.*")

QUITE a few varieties have animals in their name: **DOVE, CAT'S HEAD, SHEEP'S NOSE** and **HEN'S TURDS** spring to mind.

ROXBURY RUSSET – quite possibly the first apple variety to actually originate in North America.

SLACK-MA-GIRDLE – achieves its name either on account of its diuretic properties or because of the way it relaxed the inhibitions of young ladies back in the 19th century.

TREMLETT'S BITTER – does exactly what it says on the tin. Scarlet-coloured and early-ripening, this apple produces a cider that's as bitter as the recently ex-partner of a lottery winner.

UPRIGHT STYRE – an old, rare variety that achieves its name on account of the telegraph-pole shape of the tree.

VILBERIE – a French variety introduced into Britain in the late 19th century, and the only cider apple I could think of that begins with a V.

WINESAP – small, tart, US heirloom variety providing great acidity in a blend.

X-RATED – some varieties have wonderfully rude names, such as **BASTARD UNDERLEAF, YELLOW WILLY, CRACKSTALK, BUSHY FRENCH, HARD KNOCK, SPOTTED DICK** and **SHATFORDS**. Yes, I am incredibly juvenile.

YARLINGTON MILL – produces a cider the colour of the rich, red clay of The Shire and, with a flavour broader than an Icelandic World's Strongest Man's shoulders, is the key component of a blended cider.

ZOIDER APPLE (said in a Bristolian accent) – a variety whose name you don't know, but that turns your mouth inside out when you bite into it.

VINTAGE CIDER

The term "vintage" in the context of cider was first used by Hogg and Bull in the *Herefordshire Pomona* of 1888 – a catalogue of popular cider apples of the time (many of which are still widely used today). "Vintage quality" in this context means "able to produce complex and satisfying flavours and aromas". So as a descriptor it is entirely based on enjoyment, rather than on anything you can actually measure.

Some cider makers believe that "vintage" should be attributed to a particular style, namely one that has rich, full tannins and has been aged to develop broad phenolic aromas.

But, I believe, the greatest opportunity is to use the term just as the wine industry uses it – to denote the product from a single year's harvest. Its most basic function, therefore, is to tell the consumer the age of the wine. But of more profound importance, the vintage allows the wine maker to express that wine in the style that befits the specific characters that are accentuated in that particular year. It emphasizes the difference between a wine made in two different years but from the same fruit – so it is actively moving away from homogeneity. And this is precisely what cider has the opportunity to do. Some cider makers already do this. These are the "orchard" cider makers, who place emphasis on varietal selection and vintage variation.

But how and why do we get these variations? If fruit from the same trees is processed using the same production methods in two successive years, how can the resulting ciders be different from each other? The answer lies in every British person's favourite obsession – the weather. The climatic conditions in the annual fruit cycle, culminating in the autumnal harvest, are different from one year to the next. Each is, in fact, unique, with a bespoke set of elements contributing to the properties of that year's fruit.

A complex set of factors intertwine to create each year's growing conditions, but there are some major ones we can look at. First, there is the crucial blossom period. In the spring, Mother Nature puts on a riotously beautiful show, with hedgerow trees and fruiting trees sporting their delicate flowers for pollination.

Unlike stone fruits such as peaches and nectarines, top fruits such as apples are almost always self-infertile. This means that you need pollen from another variety to cross-pollinate with every apple tree in order for fruit to be formed.

This pollination process is largely undertaken by insects, who are encouraged by warm, dry weather – it makes orchards

OPPOSITE: There are well over a hundred different UK cider-apple varieties, each with their own unique shapes, sizes, colours, properties and characteristics.

BELOW: The concept of "vintage" is starting to gain some traction within the cider world (where it is allowed).

Ultimately, it's not a case of one type of apple, or one interpretation of cider making, being better than another. It's about diversity and options.

literally buzz with activity. Cool, wet weather, on the other hand, makes our pollinating friends much less inclined to come out and play. Even more devastating is when an orchard is exposed to a late frost during blossom time. This can effectively "burn" and kill off the blossom, so no fruit is formed.

Apples respond positively to sunshine. Sunshine converts starch into readily fermentable sugar, while a dry year helps to increase the complexity and intensity of flavour. A cold, wet year will generally produce ciders with less intense flavours.

Alas, around the world, there are a number of hurdles to utilizing the term "vintage". The global wine industry has a vice-like grip over terminology that it has come to use over the years. As a result, in some markets, like the UK, there are strong stipulations on how the term can be used and the order of wording. In other markets, like the US, the term currently cannot be used at all. The struggle continues.

TERROIR AND OTHER FACTORS

Vintage variation only tells part of the story, however. The specific location where the fruit is grown and where the cider is made will also have a massive hold over the potential characteristics of the resultant cider.

For example, a Dabinett cider made in Herefordshire will taste a bit different to one made in Somerset. In fact, a Dabinett cider from East Somerset will taste different to one from West Somerset. In faaaact, Dabinett made from trees on opposing sides of the same valley could potentially produce a different taste.

If we were talking about wine, we would call this *terroir*. Some locations have a certain combination of geographical factors that lend themselves to producing more finessed and interesting ciders than others. In wine, this concept has been understood for centuries, and as far back as 1664 the Englishman clergyman Dr John Beale was writing this account of West Country cider:

> He that would treat exactly of Cider
> and Perry, must lay his foundation
> so deep as to begin with the Soyl:
> For as no Culture or Graffs will exalt
> the French Wines to compare with
> the Wines of Greece, Canaries, and
> Montefiasco; so neither will the Cider
> of Bromyard and Ledbury equal that of
> Ham lacy, and Kings-Capell, in the same
> small County of Hereford.

As Dr Beale so accurately points out, what's going on below ground is massively significant. The nature and properties of the soil – the minerals, nutrients and water content – are crucial determinants of the quality of the cider it produces.

Then there is the topography of an orchard. As any green-fingered person will tell you, there is a massive difference between growing on a northern or a southern face (with the result being determined by one's hemisphere!). The exposure will also have a bearing, whether that be high up on an exposed face or down low in a frost pocket.

CIDER APPLES ARE NOT THE ONLY FRUIT

It would be churlish, however, to think that all cider makers have access to tannic, or bold heirloom apples. It is also crucial to consider that cider makers away from the "old world" might not actually want to use these apple varieties. The flavours they produce can be so alien, and downright challenging, to many palates in the "new world", that many cider makers look for other types of fruit.

Dessert apples, those varieties grown for domestic or export markets, are in abundance in the temperate zones of the world. These

apples tend to have low or no tannin, but have varying degrees of acidity and fruitiness. As with cider apples, there are thousands of varieties of dessert apples, each with their own individual flavours and characteristics.

It is these apple varieties that form the basis of "modern cider". Rather than a pure expression of *terroir*, developed through varietal selection, vintage characters and long maturation (aka orchard ciders), these ciders often exude a lightness, exuberance and freshness, both in terms of flavour and their presentation. These are contemporary, young and often urban ciders, borne less out of the land and more out of a modern culture influenced by both craft beer and craft gin.

Often they are made with fruit that has come from the cold store rather than directly from the tree. This enables fermentations to be established throughout the year – more like beer than like wine. Not only is this an incredibly efficient/profitable method of making cider, but such is the delicacy (and sometimes downright blandness) of some of the dessert apples being used, that short fermentation and maturation is actually beneficial to the retention of the light, lean acids and ester-based aromas.

For some producers of "modern cider" around the world, the apple isn't even necessarily the star of the show. Say it quietly in Somerset, but sometimes the fermented apple is a vehicle for bold and wild experimentation with a plethora of fruits, herbs, spices, hops, etc.

Ultimately, it's not a case of one type of apple, or one interpretation of cider making being better than another. It's about diversity and options. Sometimes we want to drink a Beaujolais Nouveau, sometimes we want a 40-year-old Barolo. Sometimes we want a Chocolate Porter, sometimes we want a crisp Pilsner. There are many exceedingly boring modern ciders on the shelves around the world, but equally, should a tannic cider that smells and tastes like the cheese counter at a French supermarket be considered any "better"? Welcome to the world of consumer choice. We now just need to let the consumer know that this choice exists.

BELOW, LEFT: Bees are crucial pollinators in orchards, and their activity in the spring can have a large determination over what happens in the autumn.

BELOW, RIGHT: The weather through the course of the growing year will have a significant impact on the type and size of apple harvest.

5

ORCHARDS

Orchards are lush. They really are the most special and unique environments, on the front line of the interplay between the natural and anthropic worlds. It's as if humans and Mother Nature were entering into a joint venture for mutual gain.

Cider-apple orchards are more than simply productive pieces of land – they are entwined into the local culture and heritage.

What we must remember, of course, is that orchards are inherently unnatural places. Location, size and shape of tree, spacing distance and selection of varietals are all entirely conscious, considered decisions. Human decisions. But that's not to say that nature doesn't get to have her say – the quality, quantity and distribution of the fruit produced every year are certainly not determined by horticultural practice alone.

That may be why orchards are so appealing – they are managed, and cider apples are produced, using methods that have been around for hundreds, if not thousands, of years. They hark back to a different time – a slower time. The planting of trees is a sign of permanence and of commitment to the land.

With West Country cider apples – and with those of northern France and Spain, two other regions that have indigenous cider-

RIGHT: One of the finest sights in the UK – cider-apple orchards in full bloom during May.

apple varieties – this feeling is especially heightened. Cider-apple orchards in these parts of the world are more than simply productive pieces of land. They are entwined into the local culture and heritage. This is no annual crop, no commodified wheat or rapeseed that can be purchased anywhere on the global market at any time. No, these are varieties that have been slowly grown and selected over time to produce a flavour profile specific to a particular region, with only one purpose and use.

THE LOST ORCHARD

Our command and mastery over apple varieties is entirely rooted in grafting – the process of continuing the genetic legacy and replication of specific apple varieties and their characteristics.

The power of grafting literally became visible to me when I was out with Mike Johnson and the Ross Cider crew picking old Bulmers orchards in deepest, darkest Herefordshire. In the search for bold, tannic apples, we would meander down never-ending gravelly farm tracks, lined with forboding hedgerows, the Land Rover's sturdy four-wheel drive frequently coming in useful. At one particular farm, deep into a valley, we were greeted by a dense block of trees, impenetrable almost in their vigour. They obviously hadn't been tended for some time.

These apples were on the cusp of olive green and mustard yellow, with pretty red freckles dancing across the surface of the sunny side. Out of curiosity I sank my teeth into the fibrous flesh and immediately spat it out again. It was incredibly bitter! Gazing upward, though, I noticed a single, vivid, scarlet-coloured apple, mournfully dangling from a small branch at the very top of the tree. This was the last vestige of the original, desired variety. Looking around me, I saw that every tree in the orchard was the same – the final bastions of vintage quality apples slowly being devoured by the creeping yellow of the Bulmer's Norman.

This variety was selected as an interstem precisely for its vigour and straight growth. But without the necessary attention and pruning, these desirable characteristics can also cause the Bulmer's Norman to be predatory. It will happily throw out sports, daring anyone to deny it the opportunity to grow bigger and stronger – a bit like Audrey II from *Little Shop of Horrors*. Left to its own devices, it will outcompete the often placid and gentle-growing chosen varietal, smothering it until there is but a single red apple aloft – or, eventually, none.

I rather like post-apocalyptic movies. But they always focus on the urban environment

RIGHT: There are entire orchards across the West of England that have fallen victim to the voracious appetite of the Bulmer's Norman.

ORCHARD

/ˈɔːtʃəd/

Noun

A minimum of five trees within a contained land parcel.

and how nature (birch trees and deer, mostly – and zombies) has reclaimed the previously bustling human spaces. But what about the orchards? They'll just be a sea of Bulmer's Normans. Oh well, bitter cider will probably be the least of my problems when the end of the world arrives...

SUSTAINABLE LANDSCAPES

Mention the word "sustainable" or "sustainability" and many people will roll their eyes. Probably because they've heard the terms being used in a macro context, attached to issues which seem entirely out of an individual's control, or without any clearly defined meaning. But in its most basic sense, to sustain means to uphold or to keep at the same rate. In the context of the wider world, for something to be "sustainable" it has to operate and function in a net positive way in relation to its environmental, economic and social interactions. This translates to "do stuff that we can continue to do in the future without harming other stuff". See? Easy!

The reason for delving into the world of geopolitics is that, when you break it down, orchards are wonderfully sustainable places. And here's how.

ECONOMY We have become very adept at producing apples for eating, cooking and cider making at a profit for the grower and at a viable cost for whomever is purchasing them, whether that be a supermarket, a cider maker or the consumer. Of course, some varieties are more in demand than others and will command a higher price. But compared to other areas of agriculture, such as dairying, apples do all right. Maybe we should all ditch beef and milk and just eat apples and drink

ABOVE: Orchards are fantastic places to bring people together, promoting social cohesion, activity, exercise and wellness.

apple juice instead? This might be worth serious consideration if it were possible to make cheese out of apple juice.

But the economic benefits of cider orchards extend beyond those experienced by the grower, for they have other positive impacts, too. In the West and Southwest of

Orchards open the front door for all sorts of wild things because, let's face it, they are as close to a woodland environment as many parts of the world get these days.

England, for example, an entire industry has been created around the growing of cider apples, providing crucial jobs in rural areas. It requires specific pieces of machinery to manage the orchards and harvest the fruit: machinery developed, built and maintained by local agricultural engineers. Specialized apple contractors are needed during the autumn to harvest the fruit, while many local haulage firms will be transporting nothing but cider apples throughout October

OPPOSITE: Orchards are at the forefront of the interplay between the man-made and natural worlds.

and November, day and night. The value of orchards as a draw for tourism, and the financial contribution that that makes, should not be underestimated either.

ENVIRONMENT Although orchards can be described as *un*natural environments, that is purely in the context of them not occurring in this form within nature. That is not to say, of course, that they do not retain any natural value; orchards open the front door for all sorts of wild things because, let's face it, they are as close to a woodland environment as many parts of the world get these days. Orchards are hotspots for biodiversity. In the UK Biodiversity Action Plan – a government scheme to protect species and habitats that are under threat – traditional orchards are described as a Priority Habitat, supporting a wide range of wildlife, including an array of Nationally Rare and Nationally Scarce species. This bio-bounty is a result of the mosaic of habitats traditional orchards encompass, including the fruit trees themselves, but also scrub, hedgerows, hedgerow trees, non-fruit trees within the orchard, the orchard floor habitats, fallen dead wood and associated features such as ponds and streams. As a result, many rare birds, invertebrates, mammals and amphibians all call traditional orchards home.

BELOW: With careful management and innovative thinking, orchards can be profitable landscapes, often with more than one land use.

ABOVE: All orchards, but especially traditional orchards, are biodiversity hotspots, acting as havens for a wide variety of flora and fauna.

Of course, there is no glossing over the fact that most modern apple orchards use sprays and other applications to control certain invertebrates and fungi. But an orchard of any description will always be more bio-active than a patch of monoculture arable crop, devoid of any adjoining habitat and with a subsoil that has been tilled into oblivion. It's also worth remembering that, like any tree, apple trees are net carbon sequestrators. Through photosynthesis they are storing up carbon dioxide that would otherwise be present within the atmosphere. That's right, in order to help combat the ravages of global warming, we should all drink more cider![1]

COMMUNITY Orchards can play an important role in the general health and wellbeing of individuals and entire communities. Within urban environments, community orchards have grown in popularity over the last decade, with communities showing a genuine desire for a place to meet and rediscover the benefits and pleasures of cultivating green spaces. Community orchards are primarily planted up in previously unused green spaces, though in some cases old, neglected fragments of once burgeoning orchards that have been consumed by urban sprawl are being restored to something approaching their former glory.

These oases of green nestling among the concrete hum can provide a fantastic place for isolated or otherwise disparate people to come together to be social, active and engaged. They promote the health benefits of fresh produce and outdoor exercise, improving wellbeing and making our cities and neighbourhoods more pleasant places to live. They also offer a hands-on approach to learning. People of all ages can find out

---

1. This is obviously said tongue in cheek with myriad other factors at play – just roll with it.

Orchards can play an important role in the general health and wellbeing of entire communities.

about nature and the seasons and acquire vocational skills such as pruning, harvesting and grafting.

Orchards also have a massive social value within the rural communities in which they primarily sit. They are places that people go to exercise, walk the dog, have a picnic with family, camp with friends, steal a kiss. There is nothing better than sitting in an orchard during the height of blossom with good weather, good company and good cider. In addition, orchards are the seat of wider social gatherings – celebrations, feasts and festivals (with the wassail, an essentially English tradition, being the most prominent – *see* Chapter 10, page 194).

And, of course, for many people, orchards are more than an amenity space – they are the epitome of the cultural heritage of a particular place, a particular landscape; their mere presence is an inherently positive contribution to society.

A piece of research undertaken in Herefordshire and written up in a Natural England Report published in 2012 sought to understand the economic, environmental and social value of orchards in hard-cash terms. Residents living near the orchards in question were invited to events, so that their perspectives could be documented. One of the study orchards was on private land, with no footpaths or public access, and was not visible from any road or hill, as it was predominantly surrounded by woodland. Yet the residents local to this invisible orchard gave it the highest ranking in importance of any of those being studied. Why? Because they took immense satisfaction in the fact that this old orchard was *simply there*. Now that's pretty cool.

TRADITIONAL ORCHARDS

So what do we mean by a traditional orchard? Well, prior to the mid 20th century, agriculture in the UK was largely of a mixed nature. Farms grew a range of different crops and raised a variety of livestock to sustain the family and to sell at market. Land was precious and every inch needed to be as productive as possible.

The traditional cider orchards, known as standard orchards, were characterized by their design: large trees, on large spacings, with a high canopy. This canopy was achieved through the insertion of a third apple variety, sitting between the rootstock and the desired variety, known as an interstem or stembuilder. A high canopy ensured that traditional cattle breeds, such as Herefords and Gloucesters, could graze underneath the trees without stealing a share of the crop. Other famous livestock inhabitants of traditional orchards include the Gloucester Old Spot pig – also known as the orchard pig because the black spots on its pale skin are attributed to falling apples landing on its back!

The livestock would have spent most of the year in the orchard, being removed only when the fruit was about to fall. They would then be the very happy recipients of the pomace – *the pulpy fruit residue* created during the cider making process.

It should come as no surprise that what happens in the orchard translates into the end product. There is a theory that the best ciders come from the older orchards. Maybe

OPPOSITE: Orchards make great classrooms, as Sir Isaac Newton would surely have attested!

BELOW: A classic, traditional cider-apple orchard with characteristic large trees with high canopies on wide spacings to allow grazing underneath.

necessitate the intensive modern orcharding system (see below). For others, the incentive could be the wish to pursue a mixed farming system, encourage wildlife or simply uphold the old traditions. In keeping with these old traditions, these orchards are often harvested by hand, with the fruit being allowed to drop to the ground. Growers who have larger areas of traditional orchards can also employ the use of push-along or mobile sit-on harvesters to ease the collection process.

this is because the roots of the trees are able to tap deeper into the ground, accessing some of the rich substrata, providing a full richness and minerality. Or it could be that, rather than putting all of its energy into growing wood, an older tree can concentrate on producing fruit instead.

What we can see in the orchards from the earlier part of the 20th century is a very considered approach to the planting regime, a process known as "blend planting". Every varietal in such an orchard will come into fruition at a slightly different time. For cider apples, this tends to mean between October and December in the northern hemisphere and March and May in the southern hemisphere, whereas some varieties of dessert apple can often be a little earlier. Farmers knew not to plant a number of varieties that all fruited, say, in October, because it would be impossible to process all of the fruit in a timely fashion. Instead, they planted varieties which came into fruition at different stages of the harvest season, enabling them to pick and press the fruit at optimal ripeness, while ensuring a manageable workload. They also planted varieties with a range of characteristics, so that they could blend different ciders together in the spring to give a full spectrum of flavours.

This "blended" style of orchard has not been consigned to the past, however, with many smaller cider makers around the world using this system today. For some, this may be because they don't produce enough fruit to

MODERN ORCHARDS

Traditional standard orchards were the norm until the 1960s, when increasing cider consumption in the UK brought a need for a new, mechanized system that raised yield per acre: a process that was being seen across all forms of agriculture post-World War Two. For cider orchards, this meant the development of the modern "bush" orchards. These are differentiated from standard orchards by the sheer density of planting, and by the habit of the tree.

With the intensification of agriculture at this time, mixed land use started to wane, and crop-specific farming became the norm. This meant that blocks of land could be dedicated solely to growing cider apples, and thus there was no need for a high canopy to prevent browsing. As a result, the apple trees became much smaller; they were grafted onto dwarfing rootstocks to stunt their growth, and planted in neat rows, which in due course grew to form a continuous hedge or "bush".

The early bush orchards were put onto 6.1 x 3.7m (20 x 12ft) planting, but over the last 50 years that has intensified, with some plantings now being 5.5 x 2.5m (18 x 8 ft),

OPPOSITE, TOP: A classic scene from The Shire – a traditional cider-apple orchard in all its blooming glory.

OPPOSITE, BOTTOM: Modern apple orchards are planted more densely.

equating to 303 trees per acre. In addition to simply increasing the number of trees, and therefore the quantity of fruit, the bush-orchard system also allowed for mechanized orchard management, thus revolutionizing the commercial cider apple-growing industry.

Bush orchards tend to be planted in monoculture blocks – meaning only one variety per block – making harvesting easier, although in order to ensure pollination they need either to be adjacent to other varieties or to have pollinator trees dotted within the blocks. Only about a dozen or so varieties are suitable to be planted in these orchards. Apple-growers and cider makers alike need to have varieties that crop precociously and consistently – biennialism is a big no-no. As a result, many varieties, although revered for the quality of their juice, are not found in bush orchards. Kingston Black, for example, despite its stellar status as the source of an exquisite cider, often bears little fruit, while Tremlett's Bitter is so biennial by nature that it will frequently offer not a single apple every other year.

Dabinett and Michelin account for two-thirds of all the cider apples grown in the UK – good tannins, relatively easy tree management and good annual cropping make them the go-to varieties. However, they both come to fruition in late October, which causes a challenging spike in apple harvesting during this time and leads to some of the crop being picked earlier or later than is ideal. As a result, a new group of cider apples has been developed that ripen in early October to help spread the load through the season.

GLOBAL ORCHARDS

Modern orchards take different forms elsewhere in the world. The mechanized harvesting of fruit from the ground largely

remains the domain of the UK. Elsewhere in the world, there is simply not the culture or the scale to necessitate mechanized harvesting. In some cases, a suspicion (or at least lack of understanding) of picking fruit from the ground exists, such as in the US. Here, because fresh, unpasteurized juice is often referred to as "cider", with its fermented cousin afforded the prefix of "hard", there is often some confusion as to the implications of fruit touching the ground.

Certain pathogens, such as Patulin and E. Coli, can be picked up from the ground.

Without any microbial control, these pathogens could potentially cause harm to humans. Thankfully, "hard" cider has the protection of fermentation, alcohol and often pasteurization. However, despite the lack of risk of using ground-fallen fruit, there is still massive distrust.

The majority of fruit around the world is picked straight off the tree, of course, because it is originally destined to be eaten. Allowing the fruit to fall to the ground will cause cosmetic damage, denying it the opportunity to gain the highest grade. Where apples are being grown specifically for cider making, dense plantings of dwarf trees are increasingly the norm. Trained along trellises, these trees produce fruit very quickly and their diminutive stature makes harvesting the fruit from the tree relatively easy. In some areas, the "Y-shape" is gaining popularity on account of its ability to trap light and for ease of harvesting.

OPPOSITE: Modern orchards outside of the UK are almost exclusively harvested by hand from the tree, so the trees are grown in a way to facilitate this.

BELOW: Modern cider-apple orchards in the UK are specifically designed to enable mechanical harvesting.

6

THE ART & SCIENCE OF CIDER MAKING

The cider-making process is, ostensibly, a simple one – get fruit, squeeze it, get juice, juice contains sugar, yeast converts sugar to alcohol. Boom. Done. If you were to follow these steps, you would certainly achieve a cider (that is, fermented apple juice), but it wouldn't be a *good* cider. Consistently producing quality ciders requires a high level of skill and knowledge.

The basic premise of cider making is the same as that of wine, with the naturally fermentable sugars within the fruit providing the source of the alcohol. Yet cider is most definitely not wine. Apples contain considerably less sugar that grapes, so they produce a lower alcohol-by-volume (ABV) drink. And, although it does exist in some countries, there is no long-standing, established practice of fermenting "on the skins" for tannin extraction, as there is with wine – the tannins in West Country and French cider apples are distributed through the flesh rather than concentrated in the skin.

In nearly all modern markets, cider is predominantly served in the style of a beer – usually carbonated, on draught, in can or in single-serve crown-capped bottles – yet the cider making and brewing processes are inherently different. Some cider makers can be somewhat dismissive of brewing, naughtily referring to brewers as tea-makers who just "pop the kettle on". That remark isn't meant to be taken seriously, but there is a point to it: whereas brewing does, of course, involve a great deal of control, cider making requires the skill and technique to navigate the natural pathways and to adapt to what has been afforded by the goddess of orchards, Pomona.

So how do the two processes differ? Well, in almost every way, really:

- **NO HEAT OR MALT** Cider gets its naturally fermentable sugars from the apple juice, so there is no need for an extraneous source, nor is any heat required to convert the juice into a fermentable format.
- **NO NEED FOR WATER** Again, cider achieves its liquid format from the juice contained in the apples.
- **NO NEED FOR HOPS** With cider, the flavouring and preserving qualities that hops bring to beer are sourced from tannins and acidity that occur naturally in apples.

There are, as always, certain caveats and exceptions to the rule, which we will explore later in this chapter. But what is crucial to take away is that cider is a wonderfully versatile and unique drink.

THE CIDER-MAKING PROCESS

The seven steps to heaven in cider making are:

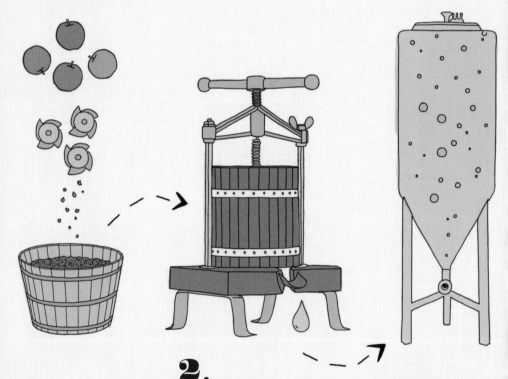

1.
HARVESTING
see page 76

2.
MILLING & PRESSING
see page 80

3.
FERMENTATION
see page 84

5.
BLENDING
see page 92

6.
STABILIZATION
see page 94

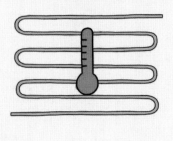

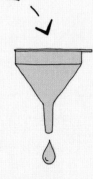

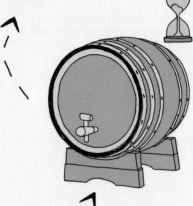

4.
MATURATION
see page 87

7.
PACKAGING & SERVING
see page 96

1. HARVESTING

TECHNICAL DEFINITION – collect apples

There are various ways of harvesting apples, based on the type of orchard, the scale of producer and where in the world the cider is being made. In the UK, modern bush orchards, providing fruit to the larger producers, are mechanically harvested in a four-stage process:

1. A tree-shaker goes through the orchard. This pretty much does what it says on the tin: on the back of the tractor is an arm with a vice which clamps onto the base of the tree and gives it a good shake, bringing the fruit to the ground. From afar, the wild flailing of the tree looks a bit like a scene from *Jurassic Park* when the T. Rex nabs the hapless goat placed in its enclosure. Thankfully, the scariest thing to be found in an English orchard is an overbearing hedgehog.

Tree-shaking looks a tad vicious, and as if it could do some damage to the tree.

True, on younger trees, some care needs to be taken, but once a tree has reached maturity, it can withstand a thoroughly good yank. If anything, the movement of the tree can be of benefit, helping to reduce compaction around the roots.

2. Next up, the fruit needs to be collected from the ground. Clever paddle, conveyor and auger technology can be mounted onto tractors to convey fruit from the orchard floor to a trailer behind the tractor. These ingenious harvesters have been designed to leave the orchard's trash (leaves, twigs and so on) on the orchard floor rather than in with the fruit.

BELOW, LEFT AND RIGHT The fingers on the paddles reach under the trees to pull apples in front of the conveyor belt, lifting fruit off the ground and into the trailer.

3. Most harvesters can't reach all the way underneath the trees, so the third run is undertaken with the blower. This, once again, is precisely what you might imagine: a glorified hairdryer on the back of the tractor, the same size and scale as the one belonging to Princess Vespa in *Spaceballs*, Mel Brooks' marvellous *Star Wars* pastiche.

The blower pushes fruit out from underneath trees, whereupon…

4. … the harvester makes a second pass to collect it.

Conversely, in traditional, older orchards in the UK and other parts of Europe, the norm is to allow the fruit to drop naturally and then collect it from the floor, or to pick it with the aid of a panking pole (yes, that is a real term – it means long pole with a hook on the end). This, on the face of it, is counterintuitive to what we know from the dessert-apple industry. But whereas aesthetic perfection (we are told) is of paramount importance to eating apples, apples for cider will be chopped and pressed, rendering their physical appearance irrelevant. A bump here and a minor bruise there are not going to impinge upon the quality of the juice that will be liberated during the milling and pressing phases (*see* page 81).

Hand-picking can be wonderfully therapeutic. All you are concentrating on is locating the next apple and placing it in the bucket. For anyone locked into a high-powered, demanding job, this is thoroughly recommended as a bit of de-stressing therapy.

BELOW: Hand-picking apples into buckets gives the opportunity to grade the fruit as you go, ensuring no rotten fruit is processed.

2. MILLING & PRESSING

TECHNICAL DEFINITION – squish apples

The fruit is then transported to the cider-making facility. This can be in the form of apple bins, bags in trailers or even an articulated lorry's worth. There's nothing quite like seeing 28 tons of apples being tipped in 28 seconds!

The crucial thing a cider maker must weigh up when deciding when to mill and press their fruit is whether or not it is ripe. If it isn't, not all of the starch will have converted into sugar, the aromatic potential of the cider will be reduced and it will turn out to be unpleasantly harsh. Unripened windfalls or tree-picked fruit can be "tumped", a process whereby the apples are heaped to allow further maturation, ensuring all of the starch has turned into fermentable sugar.

Of equal importance is ensuring that no rotten fruit makes its way into the mix. This can introduce bacteria and unwanted yeast, with the risk of spoilage down the line.

Unlike with grapes, juice cannot be easily extracted from whole apples. You have a go at "treading apples" and see how long you can last before you get bruised soles! So, a two-step process is needed.

ABOVE: The milled pulp of West Country cider apples quickly turns brown thanks to the oxidization of tannins.

OPPOSITE: Milling and pressing in action.

1. Apples are converted into "pulp", a process known as milling. Traditionally a millstone was used to crush the fruit, pushed around by a horse, peasant or naughty child. Latterly, mill technology has created a "scratter", which chops the fruit rather than crushing it.

2. The resultant pulp then needs to have pressure applied to it in order to separate the liquid (juice) from the solid (pomace). This is known as pressing. Traditional wooden presses used straw or horse hair as the mesh to filter the liquid. Modern pressing technology, although slightly more stainless steel in nature, still employs the same principles.

The pomace was sometimes soaked in water and re-pressed to create much lower ABV cider for the labourers known as ciderkin. It was also, and very often still is, used as an animal feed. Today, for the large cider makers who produce thousands of tons of pomace, its disposal can cause a bit of an issue. In the 20th century, the pomace was processed to extract the pectin for use in jams. However, once it was discovered that citrus peel had five times more pectin than apple pomace, it no longer became an economical enterprise. Nowadays, bigger cider makers send their pomace to anaerobic digesters to be fed into the mix producing green electricity.

FOCUS:
ICE CIDER

An entirely unique style of cider making that takes its influence from dessert wines. Ice ciders are characterized by the concentration of natural sugars, and the retention of a huge amount of this residual sweetness. The result is an unctuous, viscous, dessert drink, beautifully suited to blue cheese.

Increasing the sugar content can be done in one of two ways:

- **CRYO-EXTRACTION** Freezing whole apples, which are then pressed to extract a highly sugar-concentrated juice.
- **CRYO-CONCENTRATION** Freezing the freshly pressed juice. This is allowed to thaw and the collected run-off is again highly sugar-concentrated.

Regardless of the method, the juice is then slowly fermented under cold conditions, until the requisite alcohol/sugar balance, as determined by the cider maker, has been achieved. Fermentation has to be cool and slow because if the yeast gets up a head of steam it is hard to stop all the sugar being converted into alcohol, which would produce a high-alcohol wine!

OPPOSITE: Presses big and presses small, but the result is still the same – sugar-rich juice ready to be fermented.

BELOW: The cryo-extraction method – frozen apples picked from the tree are ready to be pressed.

3. FERMENTATION

TECHNICAL DEFINITION – make alcohol

Apples contain readily fermentable sugars – sucrose, fructose and glucose – which, under normal circumstances, are easily converted into alcohol by our microscopic friend, yeast.

Like any living creature, yeast is more active when it's not too cold, so keep the temperature warm (somewhere between 15°C and 20°C/59°F and 68°F is normally optimal), and the yeast will ferment out all of the sugar, creating a bone-dry base cider. The alcohol potential of the cider is determined by the quantity of sugar in the apple. This is naturally and normally between about 5 and 8 percent ABV, though it varies according to the varietal of apple and the *terroir* of the growing region.

The cider maker has two options when it comes to fermentation – keep things cultured or go wild.

CAVEAT

Some cider makers, normally the larger ones, will add extra sugar – usually glucose syrup – to the freshly pressed juice, which will take the alcohol to an unnaturally high level, somewhere between 10 and 14 percent ABV. Why do this? Well, it's not to create a new range of apple wine, it's so that the base cider can be diluted with water back to the desired ABV for the particular brand. This process, known as chaptalization, is in effect a cost-saving measure – why spend lots of money on apple juice to get sugar to convert into alcohol when you can purchase sugar to do the job much more cheaply?

In the USA, in order to qualify as a cider, a product must contain at least 50 percent juice, whereas in the UK the minimum juice content to qualify for the cider duty rate is only 35 percent. In other areas, such as Asturias in Spain and Normandy in France, where the old traditions are held strong and products are protected under an AOC (*Appelation d'Origine Contrôlée*), the concept of adding water to cider is practically a treasonable offence.

Naturally, the issue of "juice content" is increasingly contentious, with some of those making a "high juice" product unhappy that "low juice" ones are treated and taxed in the exact same way, even though the economies of scale, and associated costs of production are quite different.

The joy, and the challenge, of cider, is that there are so many interpretations, methods of production and styles of product available to the consumer. It's no wonder that there is confusion and misunderstanding. It can be difficult for the non-expert to know exactly what is in any given cider, and why one cider is different from another. That makes a strong argument for detailed ingredients listing – tell the consumer what goes into making a particular cider, and let them decide whether they still wish to purchase it if is made predominantly from water and glucose syrup.

YEAST

The cider maker has two options when it comes to fermentation – keep things cultured or go wild!

The majority of cider makers, like wine makers, will choose a specially prepared (cultured) yeast, with known habits and characteristics. There's lots that can go wrong with cider during fermentation, so naturally the priority for many producers is simply to achieve a clean, strong fermentation – converting all the sugar to alcohol without any bad flavours or aromas. In these situations it is best to use a cultured yeast that will outcompete all the others, fermenting to achieve the desired flavour and effect.

With this in mind, most cider makers use *Saccharomyces cerevisiae* – Champagne yeast – proven over the years to do the job. Some cider producers also utilize yeasts originally destined for aromatic white wines, to enhance and capture the natural apple esters. The potential disadvantage of using a cultured yeast, however, is that the cider can turn out to be one-dimensional, as only one yeast, rather than a succession of them, has fermented the cider.

The alternative, as I said, is to go wild. Of course, leave apple juice to its own devices and it will start to ferment of its own accord. This is because we are surrounded by yeasts that, given half a chance, are only too happy to start munching away on the lovely sugary juice.

First of all, living on the skin of the fruit are "apiculate" yeasts, such as *Kloeckera*, which can kick off fermentation but are alcohol-intolerant, so normally die out by the time the ABV reaches 2–3 percent. These are succeeded by more robust *Saccharomyces*

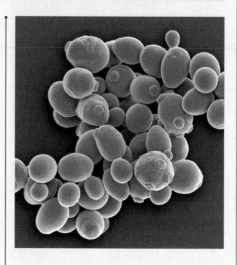

ABOVE: It's amazing that such a small organism can have such a big role in the cider-making process.

yeast strains. They do not live on the fruit, but instead colonize the cider house (from unknown origins!), living on its ceiling and walls, and on the cider-making equipment itself. These are the "house yeasts" and are crucial in the expression of particular ciders.

The disadvantage of allowing wild yeasts to ferment the cider is that they do not always produce a pleasant flavour profile, with ethyl acetate (think nail-polish remover) a common culprit. However, with due care and consideration, a wild-yeast fermentation can, through the succession of yeast strains, provide a complex, multi-layered cider.

"Wild" fermentations tend to be slow, taking many months or even a whole year to complete.

4. MATURATION

TECHNICAL DEFINITION – cider sits around for a bit

When fermentation has finished, the "young" or "green" cider is racked off its lees and is transferred to a new, clean vessel and allowed time to sit and develop its range of complex flavours and aromas. This can take anything from a couple of weeks to a couple of years, depending on the type of fruit being used and the type of drink you want to achieve. Acid-dominant ciders do not have complex tannins that need softening, and, in fact, will lose their "freshness" over time, so their maturation tends to be shorter rather than longer.

For tannin-rich ciders in the West Country and French style, however, a decent

maturation time allows the tannins to smooth out – much like a red wine. That isn't to say that a boldly tannic cider will continue to improve over the years, but simply that sometimes varieties like Dabinett taste better after two or three years.

It is during this period that these ciders develop their broad aromas (and notoriety!). Time to introduce some new "wild" protagonists – a yeast called *Brettanomyces* and a whole family of lactic acid bacteria (LABs), including *Lactobacillus*. It is the interaction between these microflorae and the polyphenols in the cider that produces some of the aromas for which West Country cider is famous, including "old horse", "hay barn", "farmyard", "Band-Aid", "TCP", "leather" and "clove".

In the wine-making world, these "bretty" aromas (from *Brettanomyces*) are frowned

BELOW: The use of stainless steel for maturation helps to retain freshness – especially crucial for acid-dominant ciders.

upon, except by old-fashioned French wine makers, and if in too high a proportion they are undoubtedly unpleasant (especially when the rich phenolics move from the hay barn to the farmyard and then all the way into the slurry pit!). But if the right balance is found between these characteristics and the fruitiness, sweetness and freshness, it can make for some truly wonderfully complex ciders.

Some ciders will undergo a *malolactic* fermentation – a non alcohol-producing conversion of the natural malic acid within the cider into lactic acid. Whereas malic acid is sharp, crisp and zesty, lactic acid is much softer and smoother, and often produces creamy, yogurt- or butterscotch-type flavours.

Many cider makers mature their cider in oak vessels, not necessarily so that the wood imparts any flavour, but because the recesses on the inside of these vessels harbour the maturation microflorae just mentioned. Sometimes, however, oak vessels are used to alter the flavour in one of two ways:

- **FRESH OAK** Creating toasty and vanilla notes, much like a Californian Chardonnay.

- **EX-SPIRIT/WINE BARREL** To impart an aroma/flavour/mouthfeel of the spirit or wine that has recently moved out.

KEEVING

It is possible to create a naturally sweet cider, but it does necessitate a little more effort than normal. An old-fashioned method called keeving, which is still used by the French, creates a bold, rich, sweet and lightly sparkling drink.

When the juice is freshly pressed, a pectic enzyme and a dash of calcium chloride are added to it. All this binds together with the yeasts to form a gel (technical term – gunky blob). As fermentation starts, small bubbles raise the blob to the surface; where it takes on a brown, crusty, cowpat nature. The French call it the *chapeau brun* (brown hat). At this point, the bright, crystal-clear juice underneath the hat is carefully transferred to another vessel.

The juice continues to ferment, but because most of the yeast and nutrients have been left behind, the process is very slow. At a point determined by the cider maker, the cider is put into a bottle with cork and wire where it ferments a little more, producing a bit of sediment and some carbon dioxide.

This carbon dioxide dissolves into the cider and is sufficient to make the sickly yeast wave a little white flag and stop fermenting, leaving a partially fermented, naturally sweet, sparkling cider, normally somewhere between 2.5 and 5 percent ABV. Norman and Breton ciders are still made this way, but there are now producers all over the world playing and experimenting with this old style.

BELOW: The gel can be seen floating at the top of the liquid, leaving a beautifully clear and vibrant liquid underneath.

5. BLENDING

TECHNICAL DEFINITION – add stuff together

This is undoubtedly the cider maker's dark art and only comes through a true understanding of the apple varieties that have been used and copious amounts of "quality control". Given that a maker of vintage ciders gets the opportunity to experiment with and develop this knowledge only once a year, it should come as no surprise that some of the finest cider makers are on the "mature" side themselves (in age rather than attitude!).

This part of the process is the closest many cider makers come to true artistic endeavour. It is a pure reflection of mood, palate and style. It is unique. And that is why it is so wonderful, and why the myriad, nay endless, flavours, aromas and textural qualities of cider can be achieved.

There are no rules here – it's entirely subjective, like all art – meaning that some ciders can be critically acclaimed for their artistic merit without actually being universally enjoyed. Equally, a cider may not be particularly palate-provoking, but can achieve a broad level of popularity simply because it is more accessible.

Although apples can be blended pre-fermentation to create a cider, ciders often also need to be blended post-fermentation. This might be because larger batches are required,

BELOW: When incorporating multiple tanks and barrels, undertaking bench trials of the various permutations is crucial to finding the best blend.

or because a carefully proportioned blend of cider from different vessels has to join forces to create the best offering from the cider house.

Some producers, rather than blending to emphasize vintage characteristics or idiosyncrasies, do it to iron out the differences between base ciders, to achieve the homogeneity necessary to produce a consistent brand that the consumer can rely upon. This can be true of orchard-based ciders as well as modern ciders, too.

Unless a cider has undergone the Keeving method (*see* page 91), it will at this stage be bone dry, with the hungry yeast having converted all of the fermentable sugar into alcohol. For the majority of consumers, a dry cider is too challenging, so sweetness can be increased at this point through the addition of sugar or apple juice as appropriate.

It is also at this point that other flavours can be added, whether they be fruit juices, an elderflower cordial, a hop infusion or

ABOVE: Every batch of cider will have its own unique flavour owing to different varieties, yeast and vessel influence.

a bouquet garni of spices and herbs. The quantity and in some cases duration of the addition is, of course, up to the sensibility of the cider maker – once again, an opportunity for cider to demonstrate its wide repertoire of flavours and styles.

6. STABILIZATION

TECHNICAL DEFINITION – make cider pretty and safe

With some notable exceptions (think New England IPA and Orangina), we fear opacity in our drinks. It's probably a deeply rooted genetic predisposition not to consume anything we can't establish the trustworthiness of. As a result, we want our drinks to be bright and shiny, so they will be clarified via one means or another. Some drinks, like beer and wine, will need to be fined, which means using gelatine (cow bones) or isinglass (fish swim bladders) – great if you're looking to get some protein into your diet, not so great if you're a vegetarian. Thankfully, there is generally no need for cider to use these fining agents, so the vast majority is vegetarian and vegan friendly.

In order to achieve clarity, cider is simply passed through a filter of some description. This removes the pectins, dead yeast and any other matter that could be creating a light haze. In the context of cider, a lack of filtration and associated haziness could be perceived as being less refined (*see* Scrumpy, opposite). Granted, a gloopy, viscous, opaque cider with purple fizzing lumps in it should be treated with a modicum of caution and suspicion, but a lack of crystal clarity should not necessarily be feared. Indeed, a light haze can enhance the natural flavours and improve mouth texture and need not be an issue.

In order to achieve any kind of shelf life, and to prevent refermentation after the addition of sugar to still yeast-rich liquid, cider needs to be stabilized in one way or another. This generally means being pasteurized – heated over a period of time to kill off the yeast and other potential spoilage organisms. Or the cider could be sent through a micro-filter, with a pore size of 0.45 microns (1 micron is equal to 1 millionth of a metre, which mean there are over 25,000 of them to an inch!).

Only at this microscopic size of pore can it be guaranteed that the cider will be stable.

Once again, these methods aren't always necessary. If the aim is to create a bone-dry, still drink, then, if you're careful not to expose it to air, unstabilized cider will be fine – though it should be drunk quickly. Alternatively, if fermentation has taken place in the bottle, this can act as sufficient stabilization. The carbon dioxide thus produced – whether it be bottle conditioning (including keeving, *see* page 91) or bottle fermenting (a secondary fermentation including *méthode traditionnelle*) – should effectively poison the yeast, thus preventing refermentation, and fill the headspace, protecting the cider.

BELOW: Filters, like this cross flow, remove gross solids to leave the cider bright and shiny.

FOCUS:
SCRUMPY

This is typically a rough, dry, farmhouse-style cider that will put hairs on your chest. It is characterized by concentrations of acetic acid, ethyl acetate and an assortment of other flavours that would be considered flaws in many areas. Scrumpy, however, is still often a preferred style among the traditional cider consumers of Somerset, Devon and Dorset.

You could describe it as minimal-intervention cider. Well, zero-intervention, actually, beyond placing the cider into a barrel for fermentation. Generally, it isn't given a lot of attention during fermentation and maturation and little effort is made to clarify it.

The etymology of the name is that this is cider made from "scrump" apples – withered

ABOVE: Though sometimes derided, scrumpy is part of the cultural heritage of the Southwest of England.

or undersized ones. Another theory of the name's origin refers to the fact that, historically, these ciders would have been made by nefarious characters, who stole apples from nearby orchards under the cover of darkness – an act known as "scrumping".

Today, in many parts of the world, the term scrumpy is used to indicate a cider with a high level of alcohol.

7. PACKAGING & SERVING

TECHNICAL DEFINITION – getting cider inside yer

Again, like wine, cider will naturally emerge as a still product. In various parts of the world a still, bottled "table" cider is produced to be enjoyed with a meal or simply with a piece of bread the size of a doorstep and a hunk of mature Cheddar that could sink the *Titanic*.

Of late, a popular method of packaging for traditional cider makers has been the "bag-in-box" (BIB). At 5, 10 or 20 litres (about 9, 17½ or 35 pints), it provides a neat mode of dispense for still, draught cider which, if kept cool and poured properly, means the drink will keep for a number of weeks.

The vast majority of consumers, however, expect their ciders to be sparkling. A natural sparkle can be achieved through an in-bottle fermentation or keeving (*see* page 91), producing a softer bubble, but also leaving a yeast deposit that not everyone appreciates (unless it is taken through the full *méthode traditionnelle* or Champagne method). But the sparkle is more frequently achieved through an injection of carbon dioxide.

Most carbonated cider is sold in kegs (for draught serve) or in bottles or cans. The popularity of 330-ml (12-oz) cans is on the rise in both the on and off licensed trades, owing to their ease of storing and diminutive size, enabling a greater range of products to be stocked. That said, the vast majority of packed cider is still sold in bottles.

Draught cider is served in typical beer measures: halves, handles and pints. However, with bottled cider, depending on the style and quality, a tulip, or any glass with breadth in the middle and then tapering at the top, will present the drink better and allow the full breadth of flavours and aromas to be showcased.

Serving temperature is also crucial to cider's presentation. The great array of subtle aromas can be lost or obfuscated if it is over-chilled. On the other hand, most consumers would find room-temperature cider unpalatable and not as refreshing as they would like.

At home, therefore, treat cider much as you would a white wine, such as Pinot Gris or

LEFT: Cider can be served fresh, straight from the barrel, but is best consumed within 72 hours if served this way

OPPOSITE: The majority of cider is packaged like beer; in kegs, cans or bottles with a shelf life of up to two years.

Gewurztraminer: take it out of the refrigerator and put it on the side, open it and then keep going back to it.

For all that cider can have a complexity similar to that of wine, relatively speaking it lacks alcohol, and this brings cellaring implications. One of the main reasons why good wine ages well is the protection afforded by its high alcohol content. Without such protection, most ciders become oxidized after a very few years. However, rich, robust and highly tannic ciders can potentially be cellared for up to five years, softening and mellowing with the passage of time.

RIGHT: The top speed lines can fill over 60,000 cans per hour!

BELOW: Bottle-fermented cider being "riddled" to move the yeast down to the neck of the bottle prior to being removed by disgorging.

WHEN CIDER GOES BAD

The old saying goes, "it's easy to make bad cider, but hard to make good cider". Here's a quick rundown of some of the most common ailments afflicting cider, why they happen and what can be done to avoid them.

ACETIFICATION

The most common cider fault, acetification is the process of cider turning into vinegar (acetic acid). Various members of the *Acetobacter* family of bacteria will, if given the opportunity, turn alcohol into vinegar. This flavour characteristic is quite common in many West Country ciders, and is an essential component of rough "scrumpy" types.

To ensure a clean, fresh cider, the liquid needs to be kept under lock and key. Air is the enemy! Acetification occurs when it is allowed in. It's simply a case of looking after your cider.

SULPHIDES

Yeasts get stressed too, you know. Not from a fast-paced, high-pressure work culture like humans. No, the source of their stress is a little simpler: they get hungry. When yeasts aren't fed the correct nutrients (nitrogen and B vitamins), they throw their toys out the pram and start producing some unpleasant flavours and aromas.

These start as hydrogen sulphide (H_2S), more commonly known as rotten eggs. Everyone loves an eggy cider, right? If the H_2S isn't treated, it can turn into the more complex disulphides, giving a wonderful bouquet of dirty drains and rotten cabbages.

So, feed your yeasts and keep them happy!

MOUSE

There are many members of the *Lactobacillus* family that can become involved with cider to produce some funky aromas and flavours. When a cider has a particularly high pH level (that is, it isn't acidic at all), it becomes more susceptible to the action of these bacteria, with one end result being rather unpleasant. An infection can occur whereby a rich, musty, lingering, acrid flavour can be detected at the back of the throat. It is called mouse, because the cider is said to taste like the bottom of a mouse cage.

I'm grateful every day that I wasn't the person who had to test the theory!

ISOVALERIC

Every cheese-lover's dream! Isovaleric acid is formed by yeast from apple-derived fatty acids during fermentation. It can also be produced by wild yeasts during maturation. When present at low concentrations its flavour contributes to the cider's complexity, but at higher levels it imparts an odour of stale cheese or sweaty socks!

I was once responsible for creating 86,000 litres (23,700 gallons) of cider that had the wonderful aromatic quality of ripe Gorgonzola. Needless to say my employer wasn't happy!

BUTYRIC

Caused by bacterial interactions with the naturally occurring apple acids, butyric acid can impart a putrid aroma and taste, often likened to baby vomit! Ensuring that you use clean fruit, with minimal bacterial load, will prevent it from forming.

MAKE YOUR OWN CIDER

Many people have an apple tree in their garden. It may be one that they have planted themselves for ornamental purposes, or an older tree of an unknown variety.

But how often is the fruit of this tree actually put to good use? Sometimes the incentive isn't there, especially if the apples are too sharp or bitter to eat. Frequently, however, in our hectic lives, this fruit lies unwanted, rotting on the ground or providing food for the birds and the beasts. Well, why allow perfectly good fruit go to waste when you can enjoy its wonderful fermented bounty? Cider making is essentially an easy process that can be done in the comfort of your own home. You need just a few simple pieces of equipment to turn a wealth of unwanted apples into their ultimate form – glorious cider.

1. SELECTING THE APPLES

As we have seen, any apple can be used for making cider, but it must be accepted that nature will determine what the flavour profile will end up like. To make the best cider, you need to ensure that the fruit is ripe. This can be done with a simple prod test – when you can leave an indentation in the skin with your thumbnail, they're ready to go. Importantly, also, the fruit needs to be clean, so as to not introduce spoilage bacteria. You don't want

any mud or bird poo, so wash your apples with a hose pipe or by dunking them into a bucket of water.

2. JUICE EXTRACTION

This step of the home cider-making process is probably the most challenging because of the need for some equipment and/or elbow grease. Ideally you will have access to an apple mill – a contraption designed to crush, chop or chew the apples into a pulp. If you're making a very small quantity of cider, you can do this by simply halving apples and popping them into a food processor, using the coarsest blade. This, however, is quite laborious (not to mention messy).

The other very simple option is to place the fruit into a bucket, known as a "trub", and

RIGHT: Inspected and washed apples are quartered before being fed through a hand-cranked scratter to chop the apples into a pulp.

OPPOSITE, LEFT: Building the cheese on a small pack press.

OPPOSITE, RIGHT: The application of pressure releases the sugar-rich apple juice.

pound it with a big pole until it turns into a pulp. This pulp now needs to be squeezed, or pressed, in order to separate juice from the solid component, which is not wanted. This is done by applying pressure to the pulp and straining the juice through a suitable medium.

The most basic form of kit for this part of the process is a basket press, which you can buy fairly cheaply and easily. If making a slightly larger amount of cider, a small pack press would be best. No matter what press type, the premise is the same: to exert pressure. The squeezed pulp releases the juice, which passes through a cloth, ensuring a most satisfying flow of juice which can be collected in a bucket or jug.

3. FERMENTATION & MATURATION

First, choose a fermenting vessel. If you are making a small quantity, a 4.5-litre (1-gallon) demijohn is ideal. For a larger quantity, you may wish to use a 25-litre (6.6-gallon) plastic container. When you use a basket press, you would hope to achieve a 50 percent juice yield: that is to say that every 10kg (22lb) of fruit pulped and pressed will equate to 5 litres (9 pints) of juice.

Ensure your container is free of detritus, sterilized and rinsed before pouring in your juice. Two choices now present themselves – either allow a "wild" fermentation to occur, or add a cultured yeast. Either way, it is advisable to add a small quantity of sulphur dioxide to your juice, to give it some protection from spoilage bacteria and yeast. Be sure to add no more than 100ppm (check the concentration before using tablets or powder). Place your fermentation vessel into a cool/mild environment with little temperature fluctuation (between 12–15°C/53–59°F will be perfect). Any colder, and you will get a

longer, slower fermentation, but any higher, and the fermentation will run away too quickly, potentially increasing the likelihood of off flavours.

With a wild fermentation, depending on the temperature, it might be a few days before your cider shows visible signs of fermentation. If in any doubt, add a cultured yeast to your juice. Under normal circumstances, within 48 hours of adding the yeast you will start to see the signs of fermentation, notably the production of bubbles. This is carbon dioxide – the primary by-product of the cider-making process.

Once the fermentation has started, place an airlock onto the top of the fermenting vessel. This will allow the carbon dioxide to escape, but keep the air out. Fermentation will take a few days to a few weeks if you have used a cultured yeast, but could take several months if you have allowed it to go "wild", again depending on the temperature.

Fermentation will have finished when you notice that the liquid clears, bubbling ceases and a heavy sediment deposit forms at the bottom of your vessel. This sediment is

ABOVE, LEFT AND RIGHT: The freshly pressed juice is passed through a cloth to remove any solid chunks and is now ready for fermentation.

known as "lees" and is formed from the dead yeast. You want to remove your cider from the lees: do so by siphoning the clear, freshly fermented liquid into another sterilized container, a process known as "racking". Ensure that the container is full to the brim, topping up with a bit of water if necessary. Then screw the lid down nice and tight.

Your cider will now sit in this maturation container for as long as it takes to soften and become palatable, which could be anywhere from a few weeks to a few months, depending upon the type of fruit that has been used. You can drink it from this container, still and dry, but if you choose to do so you must consume it within a few days (not always an issue, granted!). The reason for this haste is that by taking out a quantity of cider you allow air, and all its associated spoilage organisms, to enter.

4. BOTTLING

The preferable option is to bottle your cider. First, however, it is absolutely crucial to ensure that no sugar remains. **If too much fermentable sugar is present when bottled, the bottle could explode under the pressure.** You can check no sugar remains by purchasing a hydrometer. If the reading on the hydrometer is 1.000, then you're good to go. If your hydrometer reading is greater than 1.000, then you still have a little bit of sugar. You need to be certain that this sugar is unfermentable. You can check this by placing the cider into a warm place (above 18°C/65°F), where any fermentable sugars will be consumed by yeast. If there is no change, you can bottle in confidence.

Take your dry, still cider and pour it into standard 500-ml (1-pint) beer bottles with the addition of one level teaspoon of granulated sugar to each. Using an inexpensive and easily purchased capping tool, place crown caps on the bottles. The yeast that is still within the cider will enable a secondary fermentation in the bottle, producing a touch more alcohol, but, crucially, producing carbon dioxide too. This gets trapped in the bottle and will dissolve into the cider, creating a natural sparkle and also preserving the cider. The bottles should be placed somewhere cool (around 12°C/53°F) to allow a gradual but full secondary in-bottle fermentation.

5. DRINKING

The most important and enjoyable step of all! The cider could stay at its prime for at least a couple of years if the carbon dioxide has successfully filled all of the headspace in the bottle.

Cheers!

BELOW: A selection of containers with recently finished, or fully racked, ciders going through their maturation process.

STYLES OF CIDER & PERRY

For anybody who likes a tipple, there's no denying these are great times, with a greater wealth of brands and greater access to drinks from distant shores than ever before. However, this drinks revolution we find ourselves in the midst of is a pretty recent phenomenon.

Even a short while ago, most of us stayed on a fairly narrow path of drinks consumption – lagers and ales for the beer-lovers; a nip of Scotch, or a spirit and mixer for those of a distilled inclination; and crisp, fresh white or soft, fruity red wines for the vinifera fan club.

In the UK, not so long ago you were still thought of as a bit pretentious if you bought a moderately priced bottle of wine, or as a bit of a high roller if you went for a beer that wasn't a bitter or a classic lager. Choosing a single malt rather than a blend would incite accusations of flashing the cash.

My, how things have changed. Yes, the proliferation of producers of these various liquids has undoubtedly brought more range to the drinks market, but the fact is, there haven't been manifold new styles created. Belgian sour beers have always existed; bold gins and single malts have always existed; luscious Pinot Gris, salty Albariño and fruity Pinot Noir have always existed. Based on unique geography, culture, tradition, ingredients and techniques, clear and readily identifiable styles of these drinks have been around for years, and in some cases centuries.

No, what has changed is consumer awareness of the full range of drink styles out there, accompanying a new wave of modern interpretations, pushing boundaries and intriguing palates. Crucially, for beers, wines and spirits, a long-established framework of styles has helped inform the curious consumer, and has navigated them down their boozy canyon.

Today, most drinkers would be able to name at least two styles of beer, even if it was lager and IPA. What about wine? Surely everyone can name two grape varietals? Everybody drinks Sauvignon Blanc and Pinot Grigio these days, it seems. Easy.

Most pertinently, this wealth of information has also been fed to the wider drinks trade, predominantly by brewers, wine makers and distillers, but also by merchants and distributors. People take pride in being knowledgeable experts in a drinks category, even if they aren't necessarily producers.

CIDER HAS NO STYLE?

This is where cider is at a disadvantage. No doubt, there are plenty of passionate cider people about – people who know what brands they like, can tell the difference between dry and sweet, recognize that they like their cider rough or smooth. But that is not the basis of a rigorous classification of different types and styles.

If cider is going to flourish on the global scale, and turn into a truly High Value Perception (HVP) product, we need to give consumers and the drinks trade…scratch that… we need to give the *world* a cider

LEFT: The huge range of
types of cider available to the
consumer is at the same time
informative and confusing.

*We need to give the world a cider language
and a definition of cider styles that can be
readily understood by all.*

language and a definition of cider styles that can be readily understood by all.

The big question is, why doesn't such a thing already exist, especially in the UK, with its wealth of history and its being the world's largest consumer of cider? Well, the fact is, if we go back far enough, distinctions between ciders *were* being made, based on apple variety and method of production. There is frequent reference in literature from the 17th century to ciders made from *pepins* as opposed to *hard cider apples* – a knowledgeable differentiation between bold, rich, tannic drinks and those displaying light, fresher, more acidic qualities.

So why doesn't this level of knowledge, language and distinction exist today? We can only assume that, with the commercialization of cider, a need for consistency (rather than vintage variation) and a recognized brand of cider for consumers to understand became of primary importance.

As the larger cider industry moved away from its agricultural roots and into the realm of FMCG (Fast-moving Consumer Goods), it developed its own language, one born not out of variety selection, cider-making method or style, but rather out of consumer expectation and value perception. Welcome to the world of "everyday", "mainstream" and "premium". These terms assist the drinks trade to understand consumer purchase habits, but do nothing to help the consumers themselves to be more informed about what, exactly, it is that they are drinking. Except for it being a "premium" cider, obviously.

The result is that cider drinkers, or potential cider drinkers, have a pretty tough time finding a great cider experience. How many times has the following scene played out around the world? Walk into a bar today, even in the heart of The Shire, and you can expect to be greeted by a (hopefully) knowledgeable bartender and introduced to an array of beer styles, a fine range of wines from around the world, and 32 different whisk(e)ys.

"Tell me about your cider selection, my good man," you say.

"Yes!" exclaims the bartender, his enthusiasm attempting to disguise the sudden look of terror in his eyes, "We have a cider, which is, you know, a cider. Made from apples."

Or, if you're lucky, the response will be "Yes!" (marginally less fear this time), "We have two ciders. One is *dry* and one is *sweet*. How do you like them apples?"

Well whoopty do. Amazing. How can a focus on whether something is simply drier or sweeter enable the consumer to understand the plethora of cider styles available? It only serves to perpetuate the myth that cider is but one thing on a very short, sugary spectrum.

However, just because the UK lost virtually all knowledge of its cider lexicon and styles, it doesn't mean that everybody did the same. The proud cider-producing regions of France and Spain, keen to be insular, non-mainstream and to keep the old traditions alive, took the wine route. They developed regionally based *appellation* systems to protect and promote the varietal and methodological idiosyncrasies of iconic

How can a focus on whether something is simply drier or sweeter enable the consumer to understand the plethora of cider styles available?

food and drink products of a particular geographical area (think Champagne or Cognac or, more importantly, Melton Mowbray pork pies). This has ensured that very distinct traditional styles of cider and perry from these European regions have survived.

And for all the UK's jargon and modern, commercial cider-making methods, the old varietals still exist, and products are still made in a style broadly typical of the West Country. We have the basis of a style classification emerging.

GLOBAL FOCUS

No system can rely entirely on tradition and ring-fenced geography, for the greatest increases in cider consumption and exciting cider developments are not happening in the UK or the rest of Europe. They're taking place in the "new world". Australia, South Africa, New Zealand, Canada and, especially, the USA have incredible burgeoning cider markets.

Whatever they lack in cider heritage (or in the case of the USA, an essentially lost cider heritage), these nations more than make up for in attitude and entrepreneurial spirit. Why shouldn't they be making fantastic ciders? They can call upon their extensive dessert-fruit-growing industries for expertise and quality of raw material. They also have some of the finest wine-making and brewing talent on the planet, which, when combined with experimental mindset, gives them the platform from which to create a raft of entirely new, bold and downright intriguing products.

In order for any kind of style classification to be viable, it has to work on the global scale – that's the whole point. To simply look at cider styles through the prism of a single nation would be both churlish and foolish. Equally, we shouldn't run before we can walk, so this first attempt at classification probably won't capture all the individual nuances of particular nations or a great many styles. What we need is a decent foundation upon which we can start the process. Crucially, these styles have to have flexibility built into them so that they can encourage, rather than stifle, future innovation.

What I am about to propose is not necessarily the final conclusion – it's more the beginning of the conversation. From North America of late have emerged some style classifications that are broadly aligned to the following, but they tend to delve deeper into intra-USA styles rather than working on the global perspective.

CIDER FAMILIES

These families are determined by the type of fruit used, whether any other ingredients have been added and the method.

TANNIC

The ciders that live in this family are dominated by rich phenolic compounds, which are expressed in two forms – volatile phenolics and tannin. Volatile phenolics are aromatic compounds liberated through yeast and bacteria. They can be bold, spicy, funky and medicinal. The predominant character of this family, however is tannin. Tannin can be found in red wine, tea and coffee. It is expressed on the palate as tannin, providing bitterness and astringency, mouthfeel, texture and complexity.

BELOW: The selection of apple variety will be a, if not the, major determinant of the style of the resultant cider.

ACID

This family of cider is one that is not dominated by tannin, but by the other major flavour profile – acidity. The predominant acid found within apples is malic acid. It is this malic acid that provides fresh, zingy and "green" aromas. On the palate, this acidity can be detected at the front and the side of your tongue, expressed as a sharp, crisp and refreshing sensation.

PERRY

Perry is, strictly speaking, a different drink and worthy of its own classification. It is made from fermented pears rather than apples. However, given that, relative to cider, its global volume is tiny and that the two have innate similarities, it makes sense to include it within the system, rather than have it be lost and forgotten about.

Perry works along broadly the same lines as cider in terms of the presence of acids and

tannins, with flavours and aromas ranging from acid and fresh to rich and bold. But it also has properties of its own:

- it is lighter and more delicate than cider,
- contains citric acid, broadening the range of aromas and flavours to encompass florality and tropical fruits,
- and contains, to a greater or lesser degree, sorbitol, an unfermentable sugar, ensuring a drink with some residual sweetness.

FLAVOURED

In the history books there is often mention of fruits, herbs and spices being added to cider, whether that be to make the drink more appealing to certain customers or to hide faults. In the last 20 years, however, the addition of other flavours to good old fermented apple juice has become a significant part of the global cider trade in its own right.

The addition of other ingredients changes the profile of a cider entirely. The type and proportion of added ingredient, plus the way in which it interacts with the base cider

ABOVE LEFT AND RIGHT: The addition of other ingredients, such as herbs and spices, can introduce entirely new aromas and flavours to the original cider base.

provides an almost endless array of different end results. The underlying cider may be dominated by tannin or acidity, but often the cider plays second fiddle to the headline added ingredient, whether that be a fruit, flower, herb, spice, hop or barrel influence.

ICE

Again, a relatively new phenomenon, having emerged from Quebec, Canada, in the late 1980s, inspired by German ice wines. Ice ciders are characterized by the "artificial" concentration of natural sugars in apples through a freezing process. The resultant sugar-rich juice is fermented to achieve an alcohol in the range of 5–15 percent ABV, but still with a huge level of residual sweetness. These ciders are normally made with acid-dominant apples to provide balance with the intense sweetness.

CIDER STYLES

The cider families on pages 110–11 give us our broad structure for being able to differentiate between different ciders and perries. These families can be broken down further into styles, whereby cultural or methodological practices create further differentiation, such as the historical use of specific varieties of apple indigenous to certain areas, and the influence of other drinks, such as craft beer and wine. I believe there are currently eleven styles that adequately enable us to have a platform for distinguishing between very different types of cider. I am sure (and indeed hope) that these styles will be added to in the future as the category grows.

Even once we have achieved these styles, there are a multitude of interpretations of each style. And a good job too! How boring would it be if every exponent of every style of cider tasted the same? The joy comes in the endless expressions of styles and long may it continue.

WEST COUNTRY

TYPICAL FRUIT/INGREDIENTS
Made using classic, tannin-rich West Country cider-apple varieties, such as Yarlington Mill, Dabinett and Kingston Black. Varieties that bring some acidity and fruitiness are also classically used to provide softness and balance.

NOTES
This style is traditional to the West of England (and Monmouthshire in Wales), though orchards are now being planted across the globe as cider makers in the "new world" become aware of the complexity and texture they afford a cider.

CHARACTERISTICS
AROMA: ranging from fruity, spicy, medicinal and earthy
FLAVOUR: a balance of acidity, bitterness, astringency, sweetness and fruitiness
MOUTHFEEL: broad, layered and complex with a long aftertaste

FAMILY
TANNIC

TYPICAL ABV
4.5%–8.5%

SWEETNESS RANGE (SG)
1.000–1.025: DRY–SWEET

Organic Vintage Cider Ashridge

1763 Cider Riot!

FRENCH

TYPICAL FRUIT/INGREDIENTS
Made using classic, tannin-rich French cider-apple varieties, such as Frequin Rouge, Bedan and Bisquet. Varieties that bring some acidity and fruitiness are also classically used to provide softness and balance.

NOTES
Traditional to the Normandy and Brittany regions of northern France, though the apple varieties now exist in small quantities around the world, having been planted by those who wish to replicate the style.

These ciders are made using the keeving method (*see* page 91), retaining a natural sweetness, and are in-bottle conditioned, providing a natural sparkle.

CHARACTERISTICS
AROMA: ranging between fruity, spicy and funky
FLAVOUR: rich fruitiness dominates this style with soft bitterness and astringency
MOUTHFEEL: broad, layered and complex with a long aftertaste

FAMILY
TANNIC

TYPICAL ABV
2.5%–6.0%

SWEETNESS RANGE (SG)
1.005–1.025: OFF DRY–SWEET

Cidre Demi-Sec
Christian
Drouin

Cidre de Normandie
Le Père Jules

DOMESTIC APPLE

TYPICAL FRUIT/INGREDIENTS
Made using eating, cooking and heirloom apples. The predominant characteristic of this style is acidity, although some phenolics may be present, too.

NOTES
Traditional examples can be found in Eastern England and Central Europe, while modern interpretations are typical of "new world" cider-making regions, such as the USA and Australia.

CHARACTERISTICS
AROMA: fresh citrus, green apple, apple strudel, potentially some light volatile phenolics
FLAVOUR: crisp or sour acidity, but with appropriate fruitiness and/or sweetness to balance, and potentially some soft tannin
MOUTHFEEL: ranging from light and vibrant to soft and textured on the palate, but normally with a short to mid aftertaste

FAMILY
ACID

TYPICAL ABV
4.5%–8.5%

SWEETNESS RANGE (SG)
1.000–1.025: DRY–SWEET

Russet Cider
Nightingale
Cider Company

Harvest Moon
James Creek
Cider House

SPANISH

FAMILY
ACID

TYPICAL ABV
5.0%–6.0%

SWEETNESS RANGE (SG)
1.000–1.005: DRY

TYPICAL FRUIT/INGREDIENTS
Made using specific, traditional cider apples in five regions of northern Spain: Galicia, the Basque Country, Navarro, Cantabria, but predominantly Asturias. Acidity is the predominant character, but phenolic and tannic features are also typically present. Some interpretations of the style from "new world" areas are being made with domestic apple varieties.

NOTES
An idiosyncratic, dry cider style with an emphasis on being acid-forward with bold phenolic, lactic and volatile acidic aromatics. The traditional *sidra* style is still, and is poured from a height to invigorate the dissolved carbon dioxide, a process known as "throwing".

CHARACTERISTICS
AROMA: fresh citrus, green apple, volatile acidity and volatile phenolics (both balanced and in proportion)
FLAVOUR: crisp and/or sour acidity, light bitterness and astringency, freshness and fruitiness
MOUTHFEEL: light and vibrant on the palate, this style often has a long finish

Avalon
Trabanco

Sidra Natural
Trabanco

TRADITIONAL PERRY

FAMILY
PERRY

TYPICAL ABV
4.0%–7.5%

SWEETNESS RANGE (SG)
1.002–1.020: DRY–SWEET

TYPICAL FRUIT/INGREDIENTS
Made using specific, traditional perry-pear varieties typical of the Three Counties of England (see page 126), Monmouthshire in Wales, northern France and Central Europe. They are differentiated from dessert pears by the presence of volatile phenolics and tannins, providing greater boldness and astringency.

NOTES
Lighter in weight than cider, florality and fruitiness dominate these drinks. The presence of citric acid allows for a range of flavours and aromas, such as elderflower, grapefruit, pineapple and watermelon.

Pears contain sorbitol, an unfermentable sugar, ensuring that perry retains a natural sweetness.

CHARACTERISTICS
AROMA: estery (confectionary), floral and perfumed, with some volatile phenolics expected
FLAVOUR: depending on variety, can display any combination of fresh acidity, fruitiness and bitterness.
MOUTHFEEL: generally light/mid weight, but can be very bold, depending on the levels of tannin

Perry
Henry Westons

Black Mountain
Perry
Newton Court

MODERN PERRY

TYPICAL FRUIT/INGREDIENTS
Made using domestic dessert and culinary pears, these drinks
do not display the tannic characters of the traditional European
perries. They can, and are, being made all over the world, but
especially in areas where perry pears do not exist.

NOTES
Lighter weight than cider, florality and fruitiness dominate these
drinks. Like perry made from perry pears, these contain sorbitol,
an unfermentable sugar, ensuring they retain a natural sweetness.
These drinks are often referred to as "pear cider", a modern term
created to introduce the concept to new consumers and to act as a
point of differentiation from traditional perry.

CHARACTERISTICS
AROMA: estery (confectionary), floral and perfumed, with no
volatile phenolics expected
FLAVOUR: depending on the variety of pear, they display varying
levels of acidity and fruitiness
MOUTHFEEL: light, lean, clean and mid-length finish

FAMILY
PERRY
TYPICAL ABV
4.0%–7.5%
SWEETNESS RANGE (SG)
1.005–1.020: MEDIUM DRY–SWEET

Pear Cider
Turners

Sparkling Perry
Small Acres Cyder

FRUITS & FLOWERS

TYPICAL FRUIT/INGREDIENTS
Made with a base cider from tannic or acid-dominant apples, this
style includes the addition of fruits other than apples and pears,
and potentially flowers or blossom. This could include, but is not
limited to: strawberry, blackcurrant, watermelon, elderflower,
orange blossom, rose water and so on. Fruits and flowers may be
added at any time, but typically post-fermentation.

NOTES
Fruit-flavoured cider grew in prominence in the UK in the 2000s,
in the wake of the "Magners effect", dominated by super sweet and
artificially aromatic styles from Scandinavia. In large parts of the
world, fruit ciders are still associated with these mass-produced
drinks, but, thankfully, a whole new raft of bold, intriguing products
have emerged.

CHARACTERISTICS
AROMA: some cider notes, combined with the attributes of the
relevant fruits and/or flowers
FLAVOUR: cider characteristics dominate and are enhanced/
complemented by the addition of the relevant fruits and/or flowers
MOUTHFEEL: can range from light to full-bodied, depending on
the apple variety and fruit/flower type

FAMILY
FLAVOURED
TYPICAL ABV
4.0%–5.5%
SWEETNESS RANGE (SG)
1.010–1.030: MEDIUM–SWEET

Cider with Feijoa
Peckham's Cidery
& Orchard

**Wild Elder
Cider**
Hogan's Cider

HERBS & SPICES

FAMILY
FLAVOURED

TYPICAL ABV
4.0%–5.5%

SWEETNESS RANGE (SG)
1.010–1.030: MEDIUM–SWEET

TYPICAL FRUIT/INGREDIENTS
Made with a base cider from tannic or acid-dominant apples, with the addition of herbs and spices. These could include, but are not limited to: rosemary, chilli, ginger, cardamom and so on. The herbs and spices can be added to the juice at any time, but typically post-fermentation.

NOTES
Mulled cider is a popular interpretation of a spiced cider. Typically drunk over winter, especially at Christmas time, this drink is served hot with classic mulling spices such as cloves and cinnamon.

CHARACTERISTICS
AROMA: some cider notes, combined with the attributes of the relevant herbs or spices
FLAVOUR: cider characteristics dominate this style and are enhanced/complemented by the addition of the relevant herbs and/or spices
MOUTHFEEL: can range from light to full-bodied, depending on the apple variety and herb/spice type

Blow Horn Chai-der
The Cotswold
Cider Company

**Desert
Diamonds**
Graft Cider

HOPPED

FAMILY
FLAVOURED

TYPICAL ABV
4.0%–5.5%

SWEETNESS RANGE (SG)
1.005–1.030: MEDIUM DRY–SWEET

TYPICAL FRUIT/INGREDIENTS
Made with a base cider from tannic or acid-dominant apples, but with the addition of hops such as the Cascade and Citra varieties. Hops can be added at any stage, but are typically dry-hopped to retain aromatic qualities.

NOTES
A style that has grown out of the USA, especially the hop-growing West Coast, and is heavily influenced by its craft beer scene. Hopped ciders are now found all over the world.

CHARACTERISTICS
AROMA: hop-dominated, but backed up with cider notes
FLAVOUR: the cider characteristic should be enhanced/complemented, not dominated, by the addition of hops
MOUTHFEEL: can range from light to full-bodied and from soft to bitter, depending on the apple and hop varieties used

Hopped Cider
Pilango

**Hopped Infused
Cider**
Zeffer Cider Co.

BARREL INFLUENCED

TYPICAL FRUIT/INGREDIENTS
Made with a base cider from tannic or acid-dominant apples, these are ciders that have spent a considerable portion of their life, whether during fermentation and/or maturation, in a wooden barrel.

NOTES
The flavour profile will have been discernibly altered by the impact of the wooden barrel in which the cider has spent time. This includes but is not limited to:
• **FRESH OAK** Vanilla and toastiness.
• **EX-SPIRIT/WINE BARREL** An aroma/flavour/mouthfeel from the spirit/wine concerned.

Cider that has been placed into old wooden vessels to aid maturation, but where no discernible wood/barrel contents character has been imparted, is not considered in this style.

CHARACTERISTICS
AROMA: obvious presence of barrel character, but it shouldn't dominate this style
FLAVOUR: cider characteristic should be enhanced and complemented by barrel character
MOUTHFEEL: bold, rich and complex

FAMILY
FLAVOURED
TYPICAL ABV
6.5%–11%
SWEETNESS RANGE (SG)
1.000–1.020: DRY–MEDIUM SWEET

Wooden Sleeper
Angry Orchard

Barrel-Aged
Urban Tree Cidery

ICE

TYPICAL FRUIT/INGREDIENTS
Made with a base cider from tannic or acid-dominant apples, these ciders are characterized by a high level of sweetness, and typically a higher than average percentage ABV. This is brought about through the freeze concentration, and subsequent controlled fermentation, of apple juice.

The freeze concentration process can take two forms:
• **CRYO-EXTRACTION** Picking whole frozen apples which are then pressed to extract a highly sugar-concentrated juice.
• **CRYO-CONCENTRATION** Freezing freshly pressed apple juice. The juice is allowed to thaw and the collected run-off is highly sugar-concentrated.

NOTES
This style is native to Quebec and Vermont in North America, but is now being made throughout the world.

CHARACTERISTICS
AROMA: rich, floral, intense fruitiness
FLAVOUR: a complex mix of intense, rich sweetness, balanced with crisp acidity but not too much bitterness
MOUTHFEEL: full-bodied, oily, satisfying

FAMILY
ICE
TYPICAL ABV
7.5%–15%
SWEETNESS RANGE (SG)
1.050–1.080: VERY SWEET– CRAZY SWEET!

Neige Première Ice Cider
Domaine Neige

The Wonder Pear Ice Wine
Once Upon a Tree

HOW TO TASTE CIDER

The approach to tasting cider is broadly the same as with wine: not surprisingly, given that the two drinks share many sensory properties – aroma, flavour, mouthfeel and so on. It's worth emphasizing, though, that cider has a much more fun personality. To anthropomorphize the situation unnecessarily, at a party wine would be on the sofa in the corner, checking on Linked In to see who's viewed them today; cider would be sporting face paint and performing an epic air guitar to "Freebird".

Another difference is that cider is swallowed rather than spat out, because you need to detect the presence of those rich tannins that only hit at the very back of the throat and on the swallow. How can you tell whether a cider has a lingering finish and after taste if you haven't achieved a full taste in the first place?

What cider and wine do have in common is the importance of fruit. It is very hard for a single apple variety to achieve all of the properties that are sought after in a cider; therefore the majority of ciders tend to be a blend of different varieties. That's not to say that single varietals don't make fantastic and complex ciders, its just that they can be idiosyncratically lopsided on the palate.

Of course, people have personal preferences, and the great thing about cider is that it is a wonderfully diverse and versatile drink. There is a cider suited to every occasion, whether it be quenching a thirst, savouring, acting as an accompaniment to a meal or celebrating a special event.

There are three key steps to the important task of cider tasting:

BELOW: Eighty percent of the sensory assessment of a cider is done by sniffing, so it's important to get your nose right into the glass!

RIGHT: Assessing cider with other people is fascinating because each individual has differing levels of sensitivity to particular aromas and flavours.

1. COLOUR AND CLARITY

Someone far wiser than I am once said that "the first taste is with the eye". In terms of colouration, cider ranges from pale straw to deep, ruby red. This is, of course, entirely dependent upon the apple varieties used. There are no rules or expectations with colour, but it might be wise to treat anything green or black with suspicion!

Most consumers expect a cider to be crystal-clear and this is achieved through filtration. Cider naturally has a mild haze, which, if controlled, may be appropriate to the style and shouldn't be dismissed out of hand. A bottle-conditioned cider will have sediment at the bottom. Pour carefully to avoid disturbing this if you don't want it in your glass.

2. AROMA

This is critical to presenting a quality product. Even if the cider ends up tasting fabulous, a challenging or just plain unpleasant aroma means you're not going to want to bring the glass to your mouth. You can expect a full gamut of aromas, again depending on the apple variety used, what microflora has been involved in the fermentation and maturation, and whether any other ingredients have been added. Typical aromas from apples or pears alone can range from green apple, baked strudel and tropical fruits through to spicy, earthy and even downright funky.

A little bit of funk can go a long way, but it has to be modest and contribute to the overall structure: you don't want the aroma to dominate. "New-world" wine sensibilities dictate a low tolerance to these "bretty" aromas, but they are true to type of traditional West Country ciders.

3. FLAVOUR AND MOUTHFEEL

The key to a great cider, much as to life in general, is balance. Cider, without the assistance of wine's alcohol levels or beer's variety of ingredients, runs the risk of being bland or one-dimensional. But it has four heroes which, when balanced and working in unison, bring it to another level:

- **ACIDITY** Vivaciousness, freshness, crispness and sometimes sourness.
- **SWEETNESS** Palatability and softness.
- **PHENOLICS** Body, structure and complexity.
- **FRUITINESS** Richness and mouthfeel.

8

THE WORLD
OF CIDER

I adore travelling. I really do. I have always had a fascination for the wider world – its mountains, forests, rivers and lakes. But also the people, the customs, the traditions and lifestyles. The endless permutations of how we, as a human race, have managed to grow and develop into myriad systems never cease to amaze. As a young boy I used to read my trusty Philip's atlas every night, imagining what these far-flung places looked like in the flesh. And, you know, since then I've done a pretty good job of finding out, first as a youthful, fresh-faced traveller and now as a gnarled, globetrotting Ciderologist.

The great thing is, wherever apples grow, cider can be made. It is the world's temperate wine. And just as the character of wine is entirely born out of heritage, tradition, climate and varietal selection, so is the character of cider.

Take a grape such as the inland-French native Sauvignon Blanc and grow it in a dry, maritime area on the other side of the world, such as Marlborough, New Zealand: the result can be wildly different. Precisely the same is true for cider, but only now are cider makers and cider consumers truly starting to wake up to the possibilities. For example, an Ellis Bitter apple will display different characters in Seattle compared to its native Somerset, while the profile of a Gravenstein will diverge between Nelson, New Zealand, and Napa Valley.

As the world starts to drink more cider, the bold, innovative "new world" nations are becoming intertwined with the heritage-laden "old world". The indigenous cider cultures of northern France and northern Spain are opening up, allowing their idiosyncratic production methods and flavour profiles to be known and understood farther afield, providing influence and intrigue. Equally, the bold, progressive nature of markets such as the USA and Australia are providing a shot in the arm to old-school cider countries such as the UK, where the category has been somewhat stagnant of late.

This intertwining of new world and old, of innovation and tradition and of different apple varieties ensures that cider is at a more exciting place, globally, than at any other point in its history. The time is ripe, across the world, for cider to take centre stage.

RIGHT: Cider is a truly global phenomenon, not just the preserve of the old traditions in Europe.

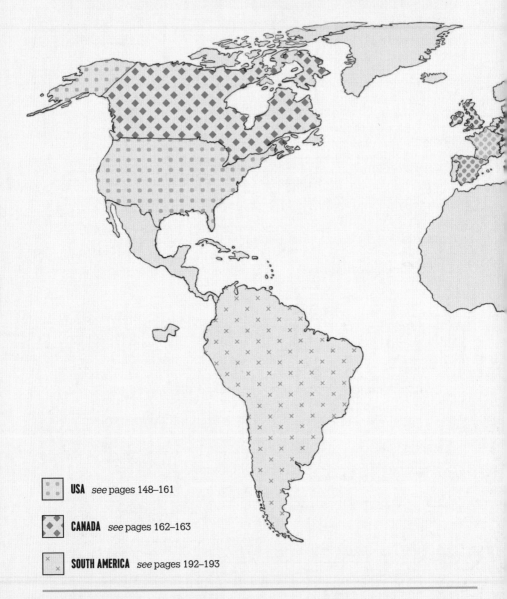

THE CIDEROLOGIST'S
MAP OF THE CIDER WORLD

USA *see* pages 148–161

CANADA *see* pages 162–163

SOUTH AMERICA *see* pages 192–193

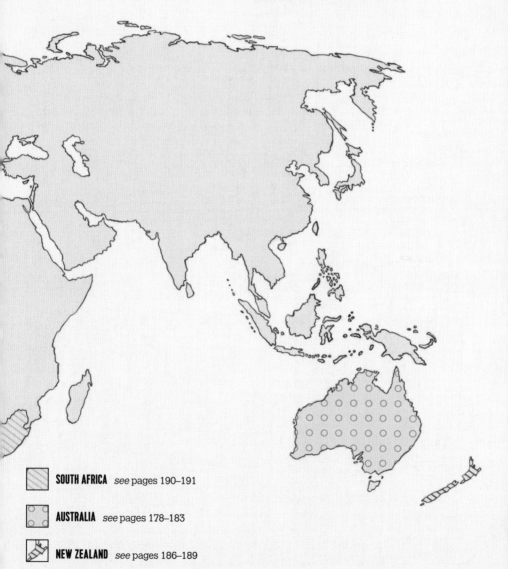

UNITED KINGDOM

Our global journey through cider begins where it all began for me: in the mother ship (aka the UK). This part of the cider world obviously has special significance for me because the culture and tradition are part of the fabric of my landscape, culture and heritage, and where my cider apprenticeship took place.

But the significance of the UK goes beyond my own personal bias – more cider is made and drunk here than anywhere else in the world. It is home to both the world's largest cider maker and numerous hobbyist and passionate micro-producers. It was the first country to establish cider as a nationally available drink – and to this day, you can go into any pub, bar or shop throughout the nation and find some kind of cider.

Despite this distribution and awareness, there is much more that cider can achieve in the UK. It accounts for only 6.6 percent of all alcohol consumed, and fewer than 50 percent of all drinkers would ever consider drinking cider.

The UK probably has a broader range of interpretations of cider styles than any other market globally: from commercial

BELOW: The tradition and culture of cider making in the UK is rich in myth and mystique.

ABOVE: The UK is home to the oldest true commercial cider making, with some brands being over one hundred years old.

mainstream, high-volume, low-value products through to some of the most exquisite artisanal drinks on the planet.

This breadth and diversity can be massively advantageous, because cider can perform a number of different functions and serve a number of drinking needs – there is a cider for every occasion. Conversely, it can be incredibly challenging for the novice consumer. How can you be expected to know which cider will suit you best when there is such a vast range to choose from?

As a result, the UK's position as the beacon and bastion of global cider is under threat: partly self-inflicted and partly as a result of the galloping efforts of upstart nations such as the USA. To quote my friend Ambrosia from the Northman bar in Chicago, "The UK is in danger of becoming the German beer of the cider world." By this she means that the UK is the high altar of cider making, the ultimate heritage and tradition. But it is also potentially the old-fashioned, the left-behind. In order to keep up with the changing world of cider, the UK needs to ensure that it remains relevant to the modern consumer so that it can prosper in the future.

Thankfully, there are many passionate, dedicated and progressive cider makers creating innovative, bold and downright tasty drinks. As long as they are facilitated in continuing to do their thing, the future will be looking rosy with cider.

THE THREE COUNTIES

The Three Counties of Gloucestershire, Herefordshire and Worcestershire lie in one of the most fertile growing regions of the UK. Their position in the lee of the Welsh mountains gives them much less rainfall and helps boost the sunshine hours. Combined with quality soils and a relative lack of large urban areas, this means that, as well as cider apples and perry pears, dessert apples, pears, blackcurrants, hops, soft fruits, cherries, plums and all manner of vegetables have been successfully grown here for centuries.

Ask Joe Public on the streets of the UK, "Where does cider come from?" and the answer is likely be Somerset or Devon. These counties of the Southwest have become imprinted on the public consciousness as being synonymous with cider because of family camping trips to these areas, TV adverts from the 1970s and the mortality-defying Wurzels (if you're from outside the UK, a quick web search will enlighten you).

But the truth is, The Three Counties, and Herefordshire in particular, can legitimately lay claim to being the UK cider headquarters. Their historical cider importance is unparalleled, with the country's most significant early varietal and methodological breakthroughs occurring here (see Chapter 3). Today, they are home to the world's biggest cider maker and have more orchards than anywhere else in the country.

Away from the behemoths, the smaller producers have retained a relative refinement in their drinks, as if the spirit of Lord Scudamore (*see* page 37) lives on in the soil. And, despite the accusations of geographical nepotism (some of which may be true), I can hand on heart say that some of the most complex, bold and downright gorgeous ciders and perries I have ever tasted have come from The Three Counties.

ABOVE: A classic cider barn, once prevalent across the region, and still upheld by some passionate individuals.

THE CIDEROLOGIST'S
RECOMMENDED THREE COUNTIES
CIDERS & PERRIES

CHISEL JERSEY
Jolter Press

THORN PERRY
Gregg's Pit Cider & Perry

LOITERPIN PERRY
McCrindle's Cider & Perry

**SINGLE VARIETY
REDSTREAK CIDER**
Newton Court Cider

ASHTON BITTER
Ross-on-Wye Cider
& Perry Company

RED OAK CIDER
Fletchers Cider

VINTAGE CIDER
Wilce's Cider

THE UNICORN
Little Pomona
Cidery & Orchard

AURORA PREMIER CRUS
Butford Organics

**BLENHEIM SUPERB
ICE CIDER**
Once Upon a Tree

FOCUS:
OLIVER'S CIDER & PERRY

What self-respecting cider book would be complete without at least a mention of Tom Oliver? Acclaimed by many as the world's most influential cider maker, he is an award-winning cider and perry maker, sheep-farmer, Proclaimers tour manager and general good guy. He has collaborated with US cider makers and US and UK brewers, always seeking to challenge the consumer as to what a great cider can taste like.

In US cider circles Tom has reached nigh on demi-god status, but he remains mercifully shit-on-his-shoes grounded. He has been making cider and perry on the family farm in the idyllic hamlet of Ocle Pychard, Herefordshire since 1999, inspired by the local landscape and heritage. The emphasis with Tom is very much on the "wild" end of the spectrum. His lack of use of sulphur or cultured yeast means that he is reliant upon Mother Nature to dictate what kind of cider it is going to be. Tom, wonderfully, just sees himself as guiding the ciders along their natural path. The result is a selection of minimal-intervention ciders, ranging from light and floral to tannic, chewy ciders.

Paradoxically to all this tradition, Tom is also extremely progressive. His love of beer has led him down many paths including co-ferment collaborations with brewers – the blending of juice and wort to form hybrid drinks to test boundaries and palates alike. However, his true passion is for perry – the ultimate expression of his *terroir*. With his intimate knowledge of select varieties, Tom is able to craft a range of perries that are a pure expression of the fruit.

DRINK IT

COPPY PERRY The embodiment of the mysticism and quality of perry, this single varietal is made from a single tree. In fact, it is the only tree of this variety known in the world. Tom has been asked the tree's location many times, and each time he tells a different lie. Good. It is the prerogative of any self-respecting perry maker to guard the location of their trees.

A still, very dry perry, with beautiful floral and confectionary aromatics, it is perfect as a substitute for a dry white wine.

TOM'S FAVOURITE APPLE:
YARLINGTON MILL

OPPOSITE: Tom Oliver (right) and crew at the cider house at Ocle Pychard, Herefordshire, alongside Hereford cattle grazing under traditional orchards.

OLIVER'S
FINE PERRY
COPPY
STILL
SEASON 2015

ABOVE: This is quite probably the rarest perry on the planet!

FOCUS:
THE BIG APPLE

The Big Apple is my favourite thing in the world. Better than my birthday. Better than Christmas. Better than sexagesimal trigonometry. It is, in short, pretty darned good. And the best thing is it happens twice a year.

This small festival has been running in the parishes of the Marcle Ridge since 1989. The Blossomtime event, as one might infer from the name, takes place in May, amid blooms of white flowers. The big draw is the fiercely contested Cider Trials. For cider makers in the region, this is the single most important competition to enter, largely because of the unique nature of the judging process: if you enter a category, you get to have a vote.

This results in 50-odd cider and perry makers being squeezed into a small village hall in the bucolic Herefordshire countryside, sipping and sampling while having a jolly good gossip with their mates. It's a sensory overload, with the sounds of cider-induced mirth and a wonderfully aromatic apple fug wafting through the hall. It's a cross between a cider AGM and a booze-up. And a mighty fine one it is, too.

The Harvestime event in October has a completely different feel to it. Spread across numerous venues, this is a celebration of the harvest, with displays of 200-plus cider apples, dessert apples and perry pears; there are also cider- and perry-making demonstrations and guided walks and talks.

BELOW: The Border Morris tradition, of the English/Welsh boundary region, is very much in tune with Mother Nature and the old spirits – there are no handkerchiefs here!

The co-founder of this event was a woman called Jean Nowell. Jean was instrumental in reviving the craft of making these drinks, especially perry, in Herefordshire at a time when so much of the knowledge and skill had been lost. She became a mentor for a new wave of makers, such as James Marsden (Gregg's Pit Cider & Perry), Tom Oliver (Oliver's Cider & Perry) and Mike Johnson (Ross-on-Wye Cider & Perry Company), and these guys haven't done too badly.

Sadly, Jean passed away in November 2017. She had become a dear friend and confident, and was one of the key people to assist guiding me down the cider path. Although she is gone, she is most definitely not forgotten. Cheers Jean.

THE SOUTHWEST

I f The Three Counties are thought of as the brains behind the UK's cider heritage, then the Southwest is certainly its soul. Here, cider is entirely rooted in the fabric of the landscape – the hills, the levels, the valleys and the farms. There is a true passion and pride that is not found anywhere else in the country. If anyone were to go to Bristol and loudly proclaim on the street that they thought cider was inferior to beer, it wouldn't take long before somebody politely asked them to go forth and fornicate.

In the rural areas of the Southwest – Somerset, Devon, Dorset and Cornwall – cider has always been far more than simply a drink. It is a currency, a language, a lifestyle, a lifeblood. Traditionally, cider in these parts didn't, and in many ways still doesn't, have the refinement found further north. The majority of the classic West Country cider apples originate from this area – some more bitter than quinine and more mouth-drying than an interview with the police (allegedly).

The resultant ciders are not always for the faint-hearted. They can be uncompromising, with a decent presence of volatile acidity (vinegar) and ethyl acetate (nail-varnish remover) accompanying the bold tannins. They can be earthy, raw, real, wild. And this is precisely how the locals like it. There is a wonderful simplicity and unpretentiousness to cider making in the Southwest. A comfort and confidence that using the fruit and methods that existed in Grandfather's day will produce the desired, traditional drink.

As with any wider region, there are subtleties in the traditions and in the varieties of apple used. But it's the attitude, the ethos and the pride in cider making that set this region apart. And long may it continue.

BELOW: Mention the words "English cider" to the average person in the UK, and beyond, and they will most likely respond with "Somerset".

RECOMMENDED SOUTHWEST CIDERS

CORNISH APPLE CIDER
Polgoon

LANCOMBE RISING
West Milton Cider Co.

FIRE
Pilton

WHITE LABEL CIDER
PressHead

IWOOD CIDER
Sheppy's

SAINT LOUIS DRY HOPPED DEVON CIDER
Sandford Orchards

THE SOMERSET POMONA
The Somerset Cider
Brandy Company

DEVON BLUSH
Ashridge

OAK-MATURED CORNISH CYDER
Healeys Cornish Cyder Farm

2015 PET NAT CIDER
Find & Foster Fine Ciders

PERRY'S CIDER

There are literally hundreds of cider makers within the Southwest of England, so it might seem a daunting task to pick a particular producer to highlight. But, actually, it was quite an easy decision. Perry's Cider (yes, I know the name's a tad confusing – thankfully the company doesn't make any perry) has been making cider commercially at Dowlish Wake near the Somerset/Devon/Dorset border since 1920.

Today, the next generation of the family, young Mr George Perry, is at the helm. Under his stewardship, Perry's have hit the sweet spot – making true, authentic, bold West Country cider, but cider that is eminently "accessible" (drinks trade lingo for enjoyed by all, including those who might only be used to mainstream ciders).

So how does Perry's do this? George says it's by keeping things as simple as possible. "We use natural ferments, Somerset apples, small-batch techniques and 100 percent juice – essentially taking the very best apples and turning them into delicious and complex ciders."

Perry's ciders also exude High Value Perception, thanks to the unmistakable "animal" range of branding. Bold, colourful

LEFT: Apple pulp being squeezed in a highly efficient belt press, producing juice ready for fermentation.

BELOW: The use of gravity and water is a very efficient way of delivering fruit from the apple pit to the mill.

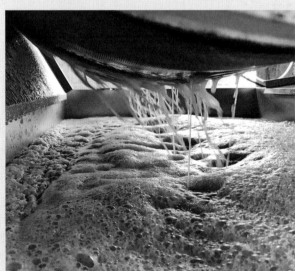

and contemporary, the labels not only ensure that these drinks stand out on the shelves, but branch out from the "traditional" cider vein and appeal to the discerning craft consumer. They tick all the boxes.

DRINK IT

TREMLETT'S BITTER SV Uncompromisingly bitter and spicy. Perry's are possibly the only cider makers crazy bold enough to make a cider from this single apple. It's big.

GEORGE'S FAVOURITE APPLE

SOMERSET REDSTREAK. It works really well as a single variety, but is also very versatile for blending, and features in the majority of Perry's ciders.

ABOVE, TOP: The thatched buildings of the Perry's home farm are picture postcard perfect.

ABOVE, BOTTOM: Perry's is one of the only producers of a single varietal Tremlett's Bitter cider.

THE ROYAL BATH & WEST SHOW

Held every year at Shepton Mallet in Somerset, the Royal Bath and West Show is the epitome of a British agricultural show. It's got livestock, agricultural machinery, outdoor-clothing stalls and dancing diggers – what more could you ask for?

The show began in 1852, but it wasn't until 1895 that the first cider competition took place. Today, the Great British Cider Championships are held at the show – the largest competition of its kind in Europe, with over 650 entries, and one of the most prestigious cider competitions in the world. To have success here, in the heart of traditional cider country, is as good as it gets for many Southwest cider makers.

There are categories for farmhouse-style ciders and perries, with products entered in glass demijohns. There is something so wonderfully evocative and uniquely British about this scene. An urbane, "new world" wine-style competition it is not, but it is no less fiercely contested or important to the industry. There is also the small matter of the International Cider and Perry Competition (which I hear has a rather smashing head judge) – an increasingly prestigious competition for worldwide producers. It truly is a wondrous thing to try ciders from France, Spain, the USA, Poland, Australia and beyond in a tent in the Somerset countryside!

ABOVE, TOP: This is what all the competitors are after – the Supreme Champion cup.

ABOVE, BOTTOM: Judging here is a serious business, with skilled and knowledgeable judges assessing the drinks.

RIGHT: The myriad colours of the ciders, borne solely from the apples themselves, presented into this prestigious competition never ceases to amaze.

THE EASTERN COUNTIES

nglish cider heritage is naturally dominated by the activities, traditions, customs and fruits that have rooted themselves in the West Country over the centuries. But all the while this tannin-stained cider making has been taking place out west, another tradition, and another kind of cider, has appeared out east.

The Southeast of England is the sunniest, warmest and driest part of the UK and this climate supports a long-standing horticultural industry. With its proximity to London, it was natural that this fruitful growing region should supply the big city with apples, pears and other fruits, providing much needed vitamin C at a time of poor health.

Indeed, because this part of England was so concerned with growing dessert apples, there was no room for another crop with less commercial value – the cider apple. This found a home further west, where land was less precious and where the climate suited its long, slow maturation and late harvest.

Meanwhile, back east, the apple crop grew and grew and, as is the way, not every apple quite made it to the London kitchen table. And in an era pre-refrigeration, what was the best way to preserve these apples? Well, turn them into cider, of course!

The fruits grown in these parts are not cider apples – they lack bold, rich, complex tannins. They are dessert apples that give light, fresh, acid-dominant ciders. In some parts of the West Country there is still a degree of snobbery when it comes to these styles, often referred to as not being "real" or "proper" cider. But that is balderdash. Yes, these ciders will not exude the same level of tannin twang or phenolic funk, but maybe they're not trying to. Perhaps they're trying to be wonderfully lean, mineral and refreshing. Remember, it's not a case of better or worse – just different.

The 290-year-old Aspall (established in 1728 near Debenham, Suffolk) predominantly uses dessert apples for its ciders alongside some more tannin-rich varieties. Merrydown, originally based in East Sussex, gained a bold reputation in the latter half of the 20th century, while Biddenden has been making Kentish cider for more than 40 years.

In the last decade, a number of new, smaller cider makers have emerged, utilizing the bounty of this fruitful region and acting as standard-bearers for this style of cider making once again. Some of these producers are also apple-growers, attracted by the opportunity for diversification that cider provides.

It has been sad to observe the decline in consumer interest in UK-grown dessert apple varieties over the last 20 years or so. There is an insatiably fervent desire, driven by the supermarkets, for nigh-on impossibly perfect, blemish-free, satin-skinned and air-brushed green and red apples. This has led to a drastic decline in the availability of home-grown Braeburns, Cox's Orange Pippins and Russets. This is such a shame. For whatever they lack in the Hollywood perfectionism stakes, they make up many times over in intensity of flavour. It seems crazy that South African Gala and New Zealand Pink Lady should be imported, with all those food miles, when we grow fabulous fruit right here on our own doorstep.

THE CIDEROLOGIST'S
RECOMMENDED EASTERN COUNTIES CIDERS

SKYLARK
Kentish Pip

TENTERDEN CIDER
Nightingale Cider
Company

IMPERIAL VINTAGE
Aspall

**BRUT VINTAGE 2016
SUSSEX CYDER**
Gospel Green

DRY CIDER
Wise Owl Cider

PEPPER POT
Bignose & Beardy
Sussex Cider

YOWLER
The Kent Cider Company

FINE ENGLISH CIDER
Chalkdown

FOCUS:
TURNERS

Exemplifying just how wonderful these acid-forward ciders are is Turners, from Marden in Kent. Leaving the hustle and bustle of London behind to raise their two small boys in the idyllic, Tuscany-esque, orchard-filled Kentish countryside, Phil and May Turner started out pressing apples with their friends and neighbours in the back garden and fermenting the juice in the garden shed.

Within a short time, they have graduated to making 70,000 litres (over 18,000 gallons) a year, using classic dessert and culinary apple varieties from the neighbouring orchards, and now have their products available all over the UK.

Their success is due to a combination of smart, contemporary packaging and brilliantly executed cider making. Turners accentuates the innate characteristics of the apples – the natural zingy, fresh crispness – making products that naturally stand out against the bolder, tannic ciders of the West Country.

"People often tell us they've never tasted cider like this – crisp, refreshing, low in tannin, really drinkable," Phil says.

ABOVE: This is a great alternative to Sauvignon Blanc for those who like crisp, dry white wines.

LEFT: Variable-capacity tanks let Turner's take cider out of the vessel without allowing ingress of air.

"Comparing East Counties style and West Country style really is like comparing white wine to red wine."

DRINK IT

RUSSET SV Eight percent ABV, unsweetened, unfiltered, unblended and unpasteurized. Couldn't be simpler, right?

PHIL'S FAVOURITE APPLE

RUSSET. It's in all Turners' blends, and they love what it adds to the mix.

HAWKES

On London's Bermondsey Beer Mile is an interloper: a nefarious, non-heated, maltless libation-creation hub – Hawkes Cidery and Taproom. With a name inspired by London's original working-class heroes, and true entrepreneurs, the street hawkers, the capital's first commercial cider-making facility opened in 2016, at the heart of its ultra-hip craft beer scene, with the aim of expanding minds and palates as to what cider can be.

Chief Hawker Simon Wright is on a mission: to demonstrate that craft cider can have as much style, attitude, creativity, innovation and swagger as any craft beer. He is unashamedly unabashed about the fact that his ciders are not tannin-led and are not from the West Country. These are urban ciders for urban consumers.

The majority of the fruit is sourced from the packhouses of Kent and Sussex, giving these unloved (and maybe slightly misshapen, but otherwise perfectly formed) apples a far more fulfillingly fermentative final journey to the halls of Valhalla than simply ending up as boring old apple juice. Hawkes has also been acclaimed for its Apple Donor scheme – the acceptance and use of apples from the gardens, community orchards and wizened old remnant trees of Greater London. For every 3kg (6.5lb) of fruit delivered, the donor will receive a bottle of Hawkes' flagship brand, Urban Orchard. Not a bad way to use otherwise unwanted fruit, and not a bad deal for the donor either, eh?

The cidery also doubles up as London's premier craft cider bar, serving not only its own wares but those of other producers from around the country too – acclaimed and unheralded alike. The writing is (quite literally) on the wall – this is where the UK Craft Cider Revolution starts.

DRINK IT

SOUL TRADER Cider maker Roberto's equivalent of a Beaujolais Nouveau, this single-variety Discovery apple cider is straw coloured with aromas of mandarin and rosewater leading onto a zesty, apple tart of a cider. Good work.

HAWKES'S FAVOURITE APPLE
DISCOVERY.

ABOVE: The cider equivalent of a Beaujolais Nouveau – drink young and fresh.

WALES

I have lived near the Welsh border pretty much all my life and whenever I am hosting a visitor from overseas, I'll take us on a little drive into Wales and, in true Dad style, will ask, with feigned concern, if they have brought their passport with them. For although the great nations of England, Scotland, Northern Ireland and Wales are (for now) a United Kingdom, Wales has an incredibly strong and idiosyncratic identity: own language, own national anthem (the tear-renderingly passionate "Land of My Fathers") and, most importantly, own cider-making heritage.

There are no particular cider-making customs in Wales that don't exist in Gloucestershire and Herefordshire, but there is a considerable number of indigenous cider apples and perry pears with wonderfully evocative names such as Welsh Druid, Betty Prosser and Perthyre.

In recognition of the uniqueness of Welsh ciders and perries, in 2017 the Welsh Perry and Cider Society successfully lobbied for the recognition of "Traditional Welsh Cider" as a Protected Designation of Origin (PDO), much like that afforded to Champagne, Parma ham and Stilton cheese. In order to use the term "Traditional Welsh Cider", a product must adhere to a stringent set of criteria, including using only fruit grown in Wales, being made in Wales and being made from 100 percent apple juice.

ABOVE: Although largely made in the West Country style, never tell a Welsh cider maker that their product tastes English!

HALLETS CIDER

There are some ciders that taste even better because you really like the people who make them. Fact. Hallets is one such. Andy and Annie Hallet have been making cider since 2002, and their company has grown to become one of the largest producers in Wales. Thankfully, they have not let expansion diminish their quest for quality.

Using classic varieties such as Dabinett, Browns and Harry Masters Jersey, among others, they aim to produce simple, honest, quality ciders. And they're darned good at doing it, too.

I like these guys for many reasons. I like the fact that they were crazy enough to plant a cider orchard halfway up a mountain. I like that Andy, like a cidery Dr Frankenstein, can use his engineering background to repair or build pretty much anything. I like that their son-in-law (another Andy) goes around the country serving cider out the side of a Land Rover. I like that their ciders have that special blend of being brilliantly and authentically made, and are incredibly accessible and easy to drink at the same time. But most of all, I like the fact that they're really nice folk. Did I mention that I liked them?

DRINK IT

OAK-AGED CIDER A limited-release, draught blend of bittersweet and bittersharp apples that has spent time maturing in ex-whisky casks. The spirit influence is not obvious, but provides extra backbone and breadth, and surprising velveteen subtlety. Big and soft. Rather like Andy himself.

ANDY'S FAVOURITE APPLE

BROWNS, because of its vintage quality and the beautiful sharpness that creates a cider with lovely sherbet-like acidity. and fresh apple aroma.

ABOVE: Based near the town Caerphilly (famous for its cheese), Hallets Cider is doing its bit to put Welsh cider on the map.

IRELAND

There's a lot to be said for taking the rugby approach to Irish cider: dispensing with geopolitical borders and considering its heritage and current practices as a singular whole.

Ireland has an ancient apple and orchard heritage, equal to anything in northwest Europe. More than 70 distinct Irish apple varieties have been identified, with many traditional cider varieties among them. One of the greats is Cockagee, which has been used in both Ireland and England from at least the 17th century. As well as making a sprightly cider, it has the extra appeal of a name that translates from Gaelic as "goose turds". Today, the predominant apple variety grown in Ireland is Bramley, providing the filling for your apple pie. As a single variety, the eyewateringly high levels of acidity make it somewhat challenging. There are some pockets of bittersweet orchards planted here and there, but the majority of fruit available for cider makers are dessert or culinary varieties.

BELOW: Bramleys are the bedrock of the Irish apple industry.

TEMPTED CIDER

Based in the Bramley heartland of County Armagh, Tempted Cider is the result of an entrepreneurial family taking on a challenging apple market.

Although Ireland grows some of the finest fruit in the world, in terms of both price and demand its apples have met with considerable competition from other fruit-growing regions in Europe and beyond. Set against this, Davy Uprichard saw an opportunity to use this exquisite fruit for its ultimate purpose – producing cider.

Having fond memories of making fruit wine with his father, he turned his hand to cider making as a hobby, with decent results, and so, in 2013, Tempted Cider was born. It's a real family affair, with wife Janet and daughters Sara and Jenni all involved.

Crucially, Tempted doesn't seek to emulate West Country styles – Davy and family simply try to make the finest expressions from the local fruit. And given that they are multi-award-winning, they're doing a grand job.

DRINK IT
TEMPTED DRY Green apple aromas lead into a fresh, fleshy palate before moving onto a smooth, mature, soft tannin finish.

TEMPTED CIDER'S FAVOURITE APPLE
FALSTAFF.

ABOVE: A very clever cider that retains huge flavour and fruitiness despite being nigh on bone dry.

RIGHT: Sláinte!
OPPOSITE: Only the finest apples will do for Davy.

USA

The first time I visited the USA was back in 2006. North America was the final leg of my global procrastination adventure, and, as I had already been bitten by the cider bug, I was constantly on the lookout for indications of the fermented apple. There weren't many.

That's not to say that they didn't exist, but as a callow youth, with zero wheels and roughly the same number of dollars in the bank account, I wasn't able to go off road and seek cider nirvana. And that's how it was back then. Cider wasn't readily available. It was somewhat misunderstood.

No, my drinks memories of the USA consist of pre-mix margaritas (revelatory) in LA, some bold-flavoured beer at Deschutes Brew Pub in Portland, Oregon (apparently it's called "craft beer" – I think it might take off) and visiting the original Starbucks in Seattle.

It's incredible now to think what a barren place cider occupied in the American public consciousness back then. Here we are, barely a decade down the road, and the US cider category is the most exciting, dynamic and progressive in the world. Some of the best ciders I have ever tasted are coming out of its orchards and bars.

But maybe it should come as no surprise that cider has rocketed in the US, for it has a cider-making pedigree stretching back further than many people realize.

BELOW: The USA has a long history of apple-growing, with hundreds of unique varieties.

ABOVE: Cider was the original drink of the Founding Fathers.

EARLY CIDER

The first pioneers from Britain into North America recognized fairly early on that the climes of New England did not easily support the growing of barley or grapes. The intensity of winter dictated that only hardy apples could survive and so, rather than beer or wine, cider became the settlers' alcoholic beverage of choice.

Later, settlers arrived not just from the UK, but from other parts of Europe, such as Sweden, France, Germany and Switzerland, all of which enjoyed their own apple-growing and cider-making traditions.

JOHNNY APPLESEED

The individual most closely associated with apples in the USA is probably John Chapman, better known as Johnny Appleseed. Portrayed in folklore, and in the saccharine Disney characterization, as the barefoot, puritanical, apple-spreading Dr Dolittle of the Frontier, he was in reality a touch different.

First, Johnny's actions were born not just out of a wish to encourage peace, love and vitamin C, but as an excellent real-estate policy. In the latter part of the 18th century, orchards of

50 apple trees or more were considered a sign of permanent occupancy and eligible for a land grant (offered to stave off real-estate speculators and to encourage homesteaders). So as a Swedenborgian missionary, as well as spreading the good word, Johnny spread apple pips, too. He moved ahead of the settlers and planted the pips in fenced-off nurseries. Not only did he reap the reward of owning the land, but he then sold the sapling trees to the new settlers, thus expediting their claim to a plot. With the proceeds, he purchased more land for nurseries and his business grew and grew. A clever fellow, indeed.

Johnny sourced his pips from the waste pomace piles that appeared in the autumn at every New England cider barn. And, as we have seen, when a pip is planted, the full spectrum of genetic diversity is explored, often with bold, tannic, sour, mouth-inverting qualities. Therefore, a considerable quantity of the fruit born from Johnny's trees could have been used for only one thing: to make cider.

Along his journey through the Ohio Valley, up into the Northwest Territory and into modern-day Canada, Johnny Appleseed helped to spread a world of apple genetic diversity which still today is uniquely indigenous and completely different from that found in Europe.

CIDER'S FALL FROM GRACE

So what happened? How did cider go from being the de facto national drink to a minor part of the US drinks market? As is often the way, several factors conspired together. The 19th century saw an influx of Central European migrants, with German and Czech nationals at the forefront. They brought with them their knowledge of, and demand for, beer, and the taste for this new beverage grew rapidly.

Most devastating for all drinks, but especially cider, was the rise of the temperance movement, culminating in Prohibition, which banned the production, transportation and sale of all alcohol from 1920 onward.

Cider orchardists were forced to cut down their trees, graft over to eating-apple varieties or keep their juice as juice and not allow it to ferment. After Prohibition ended in 1933, cider never came back: it was simply not commercially viable to get orchards up and running again, given that most apple trees take about 10 years to get into full production. There was also a lack of knowledge of varieties, many of which had been lost because no grafts were taken when the orchards were destroyed. Much easier for farmers to plant barley and get a quick return on making beer.

BELOW: A movie poster for Walt Disney's *Johnny Appleseed* cartoon.

The Great American Legend Comes to Life in Music and Animation!

Walt Disney's
Johnny
Appleseed
A TECHNICOLOR® CARTOON

It would appear that it was during these dark times, in certain areas, that a split in terminology came about. Perhaps to achieve continuity with the old orchard tradition, the term cider was kept alive, but it now referred to freshly pressed apple juice. In order to differentiate, the heathen, fermented apple juice became known as hard cider.

Today, as (hard) cider becomes ever more prominent in the US, and drinks are imported from overseas, there is a drive to reform the terminology, to drop the (hard) and come in line with the rest of the world.

CIDER IN THE USA TODAY

Significant shifts began to happen Stateside when C&C purchased the Vermont Cider Co. (Woodchuck) back in 2012. In the same year, The Boston Beer Company announced that it was taking its brand Angry Orchard nationwide.

The combination of exposure and cash that the big brewers put into cider meant that it became the new hot thing in town, especially when allied to the consumer's interest in all things "craft" – especially beer.

ABOVE, LEFT: Bringing cider back to the people! As long as it's not on a Sunday through Tuesday.

ABOVE, RIGHT: Cider houses can come big or small, urban or rural.

These national cider brands have seen their volumes and value increase many times over in the intervening years, although the growth seems to have slowed lately. In the same period, regional producers have seen their dollar share of the cider category increase significantly.

Many US consumers, faced with the wonderful range of products available to them, are now making discerning choices about their cider – and may even be willing to pay a bit more for a bit less, heralding the transition to cider as the High-Value-Perception (HVP) drink that so many US producers make so well.

So why is the US scene so exciting? Well, in an incredibly short space of time it has grown to become the thought leader of world cider. From a gathering of 20 people in a room in Portland, Oregon talking about tax less than a decade ago, the annual gathering of members of the United States Association of Cider Makers (USACM), known as CiderCon, is now the world's largest cider gathering. Well over 1,000 people gather to talk and taste. It's incredible.

Cider makers, cider enthusiasts and cider drinkers across the country are so wonderfully, geekily knowledgeable on all aspects of the drink. They talk about cider with a real passion. They are developing a language for cider, creating styles and delivering top-notch training. Most major cities now have a cider bar – a fabulous showcase of ciders from around the country, and around the world. Some even put the matching of cider with food at the top of the agenda. Hallelujah!

In my mind, there's no denying the USA is way ahead of the UK in terms of a cohesive, top-led approach to broadening the wider cider category, and it's something I'm incredibly excited about getting to know better. But (reality check time), despite its phenomenal growth, cider still has a long way to go. It accounts for only 1 percent of all alcoholic drinks sold in the US. That's less than most beer brands, let alone entire categories.

A cider maker at the Great Lakes International Cider and Perry Competition (or GLINTCAP for short – snappy!) recently said, with tongue firmly in cheek, that if you had approached a member of the public ten years ago and asked, "What's your favourite hard cider?", nine out of ten people would have replied, "What's hard cider?" Today that figure would only be eight out of ten!

That said, if US producers continue to create the quality of ciders they have been making this last decade, and continue to advocate with the same verve and passion, there can be no doubt that the industry and the heritage will continue to grow in volume and global influence.

ABOVE: Winters can be long and hard, but summers warm and intense, making for excellent, if challenging, growing conditions.

OPPOSITE, TOP LEFT: There is a huge apple culture in the USA, from fermented "hard" cider, to just good old "cider" (fresh, farm-pressed apple juice).

OPPOSITE, TOP RIGHT: Like everywhere in the cider world, this drink brings together the most wonderful array of characters and personalities.

OPPOSITE, BOTTOM: The juice, the whole juice and nothing but the juice.

REVEREND NAT'S HARD CIDER

In Portland, Oregon, is a cider maker who exemplifies the antithesis of the orchard-based culture natural to the traditional cider nations and favoured in New England. Here is a cider ethos that is entirely born out of its environment and is much more influenced by hops and barley than by apples.

"Reverend" Nat West's cider journey began in 2004 when his daughter was born and he was the stay-at-home Dad. The idea, however, of attending the Mom groups for newborns was a little too much. So he devised a different kind of Daddy Day Care.

Being really into home-brewing and gardening, when a neighbour offered Nat the glut of apples from his own trees, he decided to have a stab at making cider for the first time.

In 2011, sick of his day job and with cider on the brain, he took the plunge and went full time on the Reverend Nat business. His first 7,500 litres (1,900 gallons) sold out in two months. So he decided to go big.

The approach that Nat brings to his ciders is hugely influenced by beer. Portland is a beer town, at the heart of the craft revolution seen over the last few decades. So rather than attempt to recreate something from somewhere else, and armed with his home-brewing knowledge, he made ciders with beer ingredients and methodology. He used Belgian

ABOVE: So passionate is Nat about hopped ciders that he runs a festival in their honour every April.

LEFT: Nat's ciders are very much inspired by the Portland craft beer scene – his *terroir*.

Saison yeasts and fermented hot to get bold, estery characters. Then he started adding hops. And anything else he thought would be fun and interesting. He hasn't stopped experimenting since. Ultimately, permeating all these experiments was a desire to make ciders that no one else will make.

Nat's ciders are bold, unapologetic, flavourful, flavoursome, creative. Entirely like the Portland beer and creative scene. Talk about *terroir* – of the land and of the place. Well, the *terroir* in these products might not be expressed in the fruit, but it certainly is through the techniques, culture and ethos of Portland. So a sour cherry cider could and should be considered an American (or at least Oregon) classic.

DRINK IT

HALLELUJAH HOPRICOT This is Nat's standout, flagship cider – the one he "loves to love". He takes a cider steeped with coriander and bitter orange peel, ferments it with Belgian yeast and adds fresh apricot juice and Oregon-grown Cascade hops. Bold, fruity and refreshing – it's incomparable.

NAT'S FAVOURITE APPLE

Despite the majority of his ciders being dominated by the addition of other flavours, Nat's favourite apple is an English classic: **KINGSTON BLACK**.

EVE'S CIDERY

Based in the Finger Lakes area of New York State, Eve's Cidery is a by-word for quality, orchard-based cider. Autumn Stoscheck's forays into the world of cider pre-date its renaissance of the last decade and can be traced back to 1999, when she first fell in love. With orchards.

ABOVE: One of the most elegant ciders in the USA, this is the drink to convert wine drinkers to the fine cider life.

As an impudent 19-year-old, after reading an article about Steve Wood (godfather of UK/French apple-growing and orchard-based ciders in the US), Autumn got straight into the car and drove out to New Hampshire to pick his brains. Generous with his knowledge and gifts of scion wood, Steve also encouraged Autumn to undertake a cider-making course run in England by tutor extraordinaire Peter Mitchell. And the rest, as they say, is history.

A small operation (you can see a picture of Autumn picking apples herself on page 161), Eve's focuses very much on quality rather than quantity, allowing the fruit to express itself and creating unique ciders through the magical power of blending. The company's expertise extends not just to the quality of the liquid in the bottle, but also to the way the bottle is presented. The transparency of what goes into each cider – the breakdown of varietals by percentage and full production notes – is admirable, too. There's nothing to hide here – only pride, honesty and integrity. I'll drink to that.

DRINK IT

ALBEE HILL The epitome of the Eve's ethos, this cider is made from a blend of tannic and acid apples. It's sweet on the nose, with honey, flowers and lychee, but balanced with darker aromas like damp wood and coffee. Flavours of citrus peel and quinine hang off a taut tannic frame in the mid-palate. The finish has plenty of dusty brown tannin and bittersweet apple skin.

AUTUMN'S FAVOURITE APPLE
PORTER'S PERFECTION.

ANGRY ORCHARD

Since being launched nationwide in 2012, The Boston Beer Company-owned Angry Orchard has quickly become the biggest cider producer in the US. As with all brewery-owned cider makers across the globe, the focus is on sweet(er), easy-drinking styles at an affordable price. But unlike any other major volume producer, Angry Orchard has invested in an orchard and cider-making facility that is pushing boundaries for what cider can be.

ABOVE: Angry Orchard takes its category-leading role very seriously, and is helping to drive sustainable growth in the US market.

Based in Walden, New York State, The Innovation Cider House sits amid 23 hectares (60 acres) of orchards that are being replanted and grafted with over 60 varieties of bittersweet, bittersharp and heirloom apples. This diverse range of bold fruit, in combination with the progressive and skilled approach of head cider maker Ryan Burk, has led to the creation of some truly outstanding drinks.

A long-time home-brewer and cider maker, Ryan cut his teeth in the commercial cider world under the tutelage of former Goose Island brewmaster Greg Hall, at Virtue Cider, Michigan. Since moving to Angry Orchard, he has spent time in Europe finding out about the old traditions, learning from and collaborating with the likes of UK cider pioneer Tom Oliver.

And all this "research" seems to be paying off, given that, in 2016 (in a blind tasting, and for two different products), Angry Orchard was awarded the top prize in two separate global cider competitions. Keep up the good work, but don't get too good, eh?

DRINK IT

EDU A super-limited-edition cider inspired by Asturian *sidra*, this has a backbone of lean and mineral acidity, balanced with fleshy pears and stone fruits.

RYAN'S FAVOURITE APPLE

GOLD RUSH, a US native, developed at the University of Purdue for the fresh fruit market. It never really took off, but cider makers have discovered it and are starting to use it. It's really high in acid and sugars with a beautiful aroma – perfect to balance against bittersweet apples; it also makes a nice single-variety cider.

THE NORTHMAN

One of the best cider bars in the country, and gaining its name from being located in Chicago's leafy northern suburbs, The Northman was established in 2016 as a paean to cider. It combines French bistro chic with an Indiana Jones, shoot-out bar sassiness – but with Devon cider on tap. First and foremost, and central to its success, it's an awesome local community pub, with good food and good vibes.

It's also a seat of education, with regular "cider school" sessions, special events and tap takeovers. But this place is all about the range of cider available, and it's insane: currently 140 products from over 14 countries, presented in every way imaginable. There's *sidra* coming out of a wall nearly 3m (9ft) up, there's funky farmhouse being poured out of exquisite bottles and there are stacks of cool-as cans in the refrigerators. If that wasn't enough, they also have 36 Calvados and 28 brandies.

The best thing about The Northman is the people. I met front-of-house manager Ambrosia Borowski when she was in the UK in 2016, on a mission to discover the wonders of West Country cider. Running the bar alongside her is Cider Brian. No one knows what his surname is, because he was raised as an orphan in a cider orchard by kindly marmots. OK, that's not true, his surname is Rutzen and he's a Chicago native. And, boy, he is passionate about his cider.

BELOW: The Northman is a wonderful illustration of the passion and knowledge that spread throughout the US cider scene.

This is cider presented with super knowledge, by super nerds, offering super service to provide a super experience for the drinkers. Bravo. The cider world needs more of this.

AMBROSIA'S FAVOURITE APPLE:
She says, "My spirit apple is the **ASHTON BITTER**".

FOCUS:
ANXO

Only in existence since 2016, this project is the embodiment of all that is bright and exciting in the US ciderverse. Spread across two sites in Washington DC, it incorporates a restaurant and bar at one venue and a cidery and taproom at the other.

ABOVE: Taking inspiration from "old" and "new world" cider, wine and craft beer, ANXO is making great ciders with the utmost High Value Perception.

The inspiration behind ANXO (Galician for "angel" and pronounced an-show) is drawn from northern Spain, where good food, good company and good cider all go hand in hand. In the US, cider is technically classified as wine and ANXO is DC's first licensed winery since Prohibition. As with wines, which showcase the nuances of the myriad grape varieties, ANXO want the apple to be the star of the ciders that it makes and pours.

The company deliberately chooses to make and carry ciders (and perry) that emphasize fruit quality, expressive fermentation and masterful blending. ANXO doesn't make or carry flavoured ciders or perries, because it believes those products receive plenty of attention on their own in the US market. Instead, the company wants to show people that cider is just as varied in style, if not more so, as beer and wine, and that it does not always require the addition of non-cider fruit to be intriguing.

What is most exciting about ANXO is the positioning of cider as something to be consumed alongside, and perfectly matched to, food, specifically *pinxtos* – small plates of big flavours. To that end, there is a cider list as long as your arm to choose from, all served with knowledge and a smile. This is cider drinking for grown ups, and its pretty darn cool.

DRINK IT
CIDER BLANC This is ANXO's flagship, using local Gold Rush apples fermented with Sauvignon Blanc yeast in stainless-steel tanks, creating a crisp, dry and refreshing cider with notes of citrus and stone fruit.

ANXO'S FAVOURITE APPLE
Any with excessive amounts of tannin!

THE CIDEROLOGIST'S
RECOMMENDED AMERICAN CIDERS

HARVEST MOON
James Creek Ciderhouse

PACIFIC PINEAPPLE
2 Towns Ciderhouse

PINOT N'ARLET
Ploughman Farm Cider

GOLDEN RUSSET
Big Hill Ciderworks

EXTRA DRY CIDER
Farnum Hill

PERCEPTION SHIFT
Artifact

HARRISON
Albemarle CiderWorks

**HEIRLOOM BLEND
ICE CIDER**
Eden

KINGSTON BLACK CIDER
Dragon's Head Cider

LA SAINTE TERRE
Slyboro Ciderhouse

CIDERMAKER'S RESERVE
Snowdrift Cider Co.

CANADA

Too often, people refer to North American cider as being from the US only, as if some gigantic apple kryptonite force field had precluded the fabulous fermentation from being made above the 49th parallel north. What utter tosh.

Canada has some of the finest apple-growing regions in the world in areas where topography and water provide some respite from the harshness of winter. And in the case of ice cider, developed in Quebec, inventive cider makers can actually use the bitter cold to their advantage to make exquisite, naturally sweet dessert drinks.

There has been a modest but very healthy cider scene in Canada for years now, with the likes of Merridale on Vancouver Island and County Cider in Ontario, among a few others, leading the charge for quality ciders at the forefront of this renaissance. In the last decade, however, the total volume of cider being made and consumed in Canada has exploded, making it the third-fastest growing market in the world, only behind the US and South Africa. Accompanying this growth has emerged a wave of innovative and creative cider makers, taking their lead and inspiration from all over the world.

ABOVE: The fruit of many apple varieties lay on the tree well after the leaves have fallen prey to the cold autumnal Canadian days and nights.

LEFT FIELD CIDER CO.

Like all the best people, Kate Garthwaite undertook her cider apprenticeship with Mike Johnson at Ross-on-Wye Cider & Perry Company. Her passion and determination shone through from the moment I first met her. Anyone who gets excited about the prospect of spending three days bottling in the middle of winter can't be faulted for commitment!

RIGHT: It's a family affair... Kate Garthwaite picking apples with fellow Leftfielder, and sister, Theresa Pedersen.

ABOVE: British Columbia is not short on apples, and thankfully, many of them are now being utilized for their ultimate purpose.

Kate began making cider for fun in her kitchen in Vancouver, at first with some dubious results. She saw an opportunity to put the family farm to good use making cider, eyeing up the global renaissance just starting to emerge. But the farm is in the British Columbia interior at Mamette Lake – not renowned apple-growing territory.

No bother. With her cider interest piqued, Kate headed to the UK for a year and brought Mr Johnson's wisdom back with her, along with the idea of planting up English and French cider apples. In 2011, in company with her sister Theresa and parents Gord and Deb, she launched Left Field Cider Co.. The result: some truly fantastic and admirably dry ciders.

DRINK IT
BIG DRY Does what is says on the tin – it's big, bold and dry. Dominated by tannic, bittersweet apples, it's balanced by the fruitiness and acidity provided by Okanagan dessert apples.

KATE'S FAVOURITE APPLE
APPLEKNOTTED KERNEL.

FRANCE

The original source of the West Country's high-tannin cider-apple varieties, the northern French regions of Brittany and Normandy are home to some of the world's oldest cider making, and have mercifully managed to retain a strong cultural identity associated with tradition and *terroir*. Such is the strength of this heritage that cider and perry production is tightly controlled under an *Appellation d'Origine Contrôlée* (AOC), whose purpose is to ensure that only drinks produced from traditional varieties and using traditional techniques can bear the names of Pays d'Auge (Normandy), Domfrontais (perry – Normandy) and Cornouaille (Brittany).

Central to these *cidres fermiers* (farmhouse ciders) is the process of keeving (*see* page 91), which creates naturally sweet and effervescent products. In the UK, USA and beyond, French cider is heralded for its bold flavour, unctuous fruitiness and tongue-tingling sparkle. Unlike in the UK, where cider has become a mainstream drink, available nationwide, within France *cidre* is still predominantly consumed in the regions that produce it. The majority of French people somewhat deride *cidre* as a rural, agricultural or inferior drink. Maybe this is to be expected in a country with such a bold heritage of fine wine-making.

But the fact is, *cidre* is making a comeback. While the traditional *fermier* style becomes more and more popular with tourists, some producers are also working outside the constraints of the AOC system to deliver some innovation. Don't expect mango-flavoured cider any time soon, but do keep an eye out for *méthode traditionnelle* or barrel-aged products.

It would be entirely remiss of me not to mention that central to Normandy heritage is the distillation of cider to create Calvados – something that cider makers have been doing for hundreds of years. A visit to one of the many producers in the Pays d'Auges or Domfront will enable one to taste a range of aged Calvados, some dating back decades.

PERRY

The Domfront area of Normandy is famed for its pear heritage, and in the face of threats from modern agriculture, which would necessitate the felling of these old pear trees, an AOC-designated status for *Poiré Domfront* was created in 2002.

This region has, rather wonderfully, been able to retain a thriving *poiré* (perry) industry, with some 100,000 trees of

90-plus varieties providing 25,000 tons of pears every year. At its heart is one particular variety, Plant de Blanc. Famed for its high-intensity acidity, soft fruitiness and gentle grippy tannin, it must constitute at least 30 percent of the overall blend in any *poiré* wishing to achieve the AOC status.

Other stipulations include that the fruit must be from a named list of varieties that have reached maturity and are picked from the ground; no other nutrients may be added; and carbonation must be achieved naturally. This last point is undertaken through a bottle-fermenting process that, through careful control, normally ensures that the *poiré* returns at around 4 percent ABV with a high degree of residual sweetness.

BELOW: Spring announces its arrival with an exquisite spread of pearlescent perry-pear blossom in the Domfront countryside.

ERIC BORDELET

The name Eric Bordelet has been mentioned in cider circles for a number of years: he's revered by some as one of the finest cider and perry makers on the planet. But until recently I knew very little of him or his products.

ABOVE: Eric Bordelet's passion is for *cidre* and *poiré* that are a true expression of his *terroir*.

Not only had I never met Eric, I had never even seen a photo of him. I had started to believe that his reputation as a sommelier-turned-cider-maker was just a ruse, a character created to enhance the standing of his brand. His apparent wish to stay out of the limelight only served to enhance this view.

So it was with no small amount of giddiness and intrigue that, in the summer of 2017, I found myself with the man himself, at the family farm on the borders of Normandy and Pays de la Loire, embarking on a lengthy tasting session.

I can tell you that Eric is very real and really rather wonderful. He is, as he describes his best products, full of *charme*. Bristling of moustache, discerning of palate and incredibly generous of time, he took me, my companion and a visiting Swiss cider maker on a journey through the vaults, sampling dusty and grubby bottles of vintages dating back to 2001. OMG.

What an experience. What an utter privilege. The ciders were lean and fresh, but Eric's *pièces de résistance*, in my mind, are his perries. It's with talk of pears that his eyes shine and you can tell he really adores this drink. His *poiré* could grace the dining table of any Michelin-starred restaurant in the world.

He took me on a little tour of his pear orchards. To see these giant monoliths littered throughout the countryside was a bit like taking a drive around the lanes of Dymock. Eric had purchased a farm just down the road, not because it was a sound investment, or had a barn ripe for conversion. No, this farm had one small old pear orchard containing some interesting varieties that, under new ownership, could easily have been removed. Such is the passion of the man to retain this cultural heritage.

Eric works on different timescales to most people. He is not part of today's instant gratification culture. He is in the process of redeveloping the ruined chateau at the heart of the farm, to turn it into the most audacious, mind-blowing cider-making facility on the planet. I say that with no hyperbole. It may be ten years before it's completed, possibly after Eric has handed over the reins to the next generation. Fortunately, his children have taken an interest in the family business, and Eric is in the early stages of delivering their training. But he's in no rush. He's playing the long game, just like his beloved pear trees.

DRINK IT

PERRY. ANY PERRY. The light and fruity Chablis-esque *poiré* is a joy, but it is the legendary Poiré Granit that is the show-stealer. A jasmine-scented nose followed by multi-layered mineral complexity. Steely, but soft and fruity and perfectly well balanced. As my dear friend Jean Nowell would have said, this is "a grown up's drink".

ERIC'S FAVOURITE APPLE

"I love my children equally, and it's the same with the apples."

ABOVE: Poiré Granit – considered by some to be one of the finest fermentations on the planet.

RIGHT: Eric is a custodian of the magnificent old *poiré* trees in his surrounding villages, purchasing orchards when he can to preserve their future.

RECOMMENDED FRENCH CIDERS & PERRIES

POIRÉ CUVÉE PRESTIGE
La Galotière

BRUT 2014
Cyril Zangs

CIDRE FERMIER BRUT
Manoir de Grandouet

POIRÉ DE NORMANDIE
Le Père Jules

CIDRE
Cidrerie du Léguer

CIDRE RÉSERVE
Famille Dupont

SPAIN

The northern coastline of Spain is home to possibly the oldest, but certainly the most fervently passionate, cider heritage in the world. The *España Verde* regions of Galicia, Asturias, Cantabria, Navarra and the Basque Country hold *sidra* to be their indigenous drink. These areas are suitable for apple cultivation, protected from the intense Iberian heat by the sheltering effects of the mountains and the coast.

ABOVE: Not all *sidra* looks back to the old traditions; some are very much looking forward.

The *sidra* history here is old – very old. The Greek geographer Strabo was writing 2,000 years ago about the Astures making cider on account of there being little wine. While the rest of Europe goes into a fruit-growing moratorium during the Dark Ages, Asturian literature frequently mentions apples and cider, such as in 781, when the act of foundation of the Monastery of San Vicente (upon which the city of Oviedo will form) bears the word *pomares*.

This heritage has grown over the centuries and the legacy is still felt today in the continued production of *sidra naturale*, an entirely idiosyncratic drink, made with fruit, a production methodology and a serving style that are utterly unique.

Unlike the UK and France, where the traditional style of cider features high tannin and low acidity, traditional Spanish ciders have a tannic spine, but are dominated by a fresh and funky acidity. Traditional-style *sidra* is wild-fermented, dry, with a bit of funk and presented in a standardized 750-ml (26-oz) bottle. Rather than being poured into a large glass, it is consumed in gulps – small serves knocked backed, with the dregs discarded onto the floor.

The cider is poured from a height of 1m (3ft) or so, liberating the dissolved carbon dioxide, known to the Spanish as *estrella* or "star". This "throwing" is not just a piece of theatre to create a wonderful drinking experience, it helps to enliven the cider and maximize its flavours.

LEFT AND PRECEDING PAGES: Expert *sidra* throwing in action – not a drop spilt.

TRABANCO

Asturias is the largest cider region in Spain, accounting for some 80 percent of national production, and it has the most pronounced and visible heritage. It also has the world's largest annual consumption of cider per capita – some 54 litres (95 pints)! At the heart of this cider fanaticism sits Trabanco.

The headquarters and original *llagar* (cidery) established by Emilio Trabanco in 1925 is just a few kilometres outside of Gijón. Today, under the reins of the third generation of the family, a beautiful new facility produces the majority of the company's cider. What makes Trabanco so eminently appealing is its incorporation of modern scientific knowledge into the old methods to get the best of both worlds – *sidra* with real character and boldness, but clean and appealing to a diverse range of consumers.

DRINK IT

TRABANCO SIDRA NATURAL The classic *sidra* made with a blend of bitter and acid apples and fermented in chestnut barrels. It's phenolic and herbaceous on the nose, with a wonderfully powerful green apple zing on the palate, followed by soft dry tannins.

ABOVE: The Asturian classic – Trabanco Sidra Natural.

RIGHT: Wonderful old chestnut barrels in the *llagar*.

NORTHERN & CENTRAL EUROPE

This giant section of Europe has some considerable cider heritage, idiosyncrasies and traditions that are just starting to be known and understood in the wider world.

An exploration of Switzerland reveals a long-standing heritage of growing perry pears. Most incredibly, these trees are being grown at 749m (nearly 2,500ft) above sea level and being harvested against a carpet of fresh snow. Western Germany's *apfelwein* (cider) heritage remains relatively small, if regionally well established; its products are consumed predominantly in specialist bars and restaurants. As with many other wine-producing nations that have a cider culture, *apfelwein* is often maligned in Germany, or seen as old fashioned. Thankfully, there is a new wave of producers who are making exquisitely presented and produced drinks. Meanwhile, in Austria, *most* and especially *mostbirne* (perry) continue to be celebrated and made in the heartland regions.

One outcome of political jostling within Eastern Europe is that large quantities of apples have been deemed surplus to requirements for a particularly powerful purchasing nation. Luckily there are some enterprising folk in this region who have been inspired by lost traditions or new-wave craft beer modernity. Keep an eye out for some excellent ciders coming out of the region over the next few years.

ABOVE: A new generation of cider is being made in nations with abundant apples, but with hitherto little cider heritage.

RAMBORN CIDER CO.

Frequently the answer to an obscure question in Trivial Pursuit, Luxembourg sparks preconceptions of bureaucracy, European politics and finance, but not often cider. However, rather awesomely, there is a tradition of making it that dates back to Roman times. Cider is known in these parts as *viez*, which means "second pressing" and alludes to the fact that the presses would have been used first for wine grapes and then for the indigenous cider apples and perry pears.

ABOVE: Ramborn is doing its utmost to put Luxembourg on the cider and perry map, with immediate results.

The old tradition of every farmer having a cask or two of *viez* in the cellar continued into the 20th century. Alas, from a height of apple production in 1902, post-war agricultural industrialization meant that Luxembourgers had largely forgotten this traditional orcharding and cider-making culture. Until now…

Formed in the village of Born by three guys who reminisced about sneaking into their grandfathers' cellars to steal swigs of *viez* as boys and lamented the disrepair of the old orchards, Ramborn Cider Co. has quickly established itself as a producer of distinction.

Its most striking elements are undoubtedly the old orchards and the varieties of apple used. To see these orchards, many of them on their last legs, being restored, regenerated and rescued for future generations is not only a fantastic story, but so obviously something that is a passion to all those involved with the company.

Another big shock to find in Luxembourg is a (relative) abundance, of large, old perry-pear trees. By no means dessert pears, these varieties were grown specifically for making *mostbirne* (perry) or to be further distilled into schnapps.

DRINK IT

RAMBORN PERRY This is the company's standout drink. Fresh, tropical fruit salad on the nose and straight into the mouth. Then it goes down with a Steven Spielberg-esque twist when anaesthetic levels of astringency hit the back of the mouth. Whoa!

RAMBORN'S FAVOURITE APPLE

RAMBO, which (fact of the day) gave its name to the crazed, bandana-sporting ex-Vietnam vet character so memorably played by Sly Stallone in the movies.

BRÄNNLAND CIDER

Utter the words "Swedish cider" and the majority of consumers around the world will conjure up thoughts of the "sweetie fruity" style. Many acid-forward ciders have been produced from the indigenous fruit across the region for decades, but we are now beginning to see a range of different styles emerging.

Andreas Sundgren is the kind of guy who can't have a sourdough starter in his refrigerator without it eventually turning into a bakery. Having achieved some decent success as a songwriter and developer of a music software company, he grew tired of the disconnect between his job and his sense of place, and wanted to have a go at something more tangible.

A passion for food and drink first took him down a few dead ends: chef (didn't finish the qualification) and goat-farmer (didn't like the idea of getting up at 4am every day). A love of wine then turned him in the direction of apples and cider making, for apples grow in abundance in his home village of Brännland. With his mouth working ahead of his feet, he stated boldly that he would be making great cider from garden apples and selling it back to the local community.

BELOW: This is where the "ice" portion of ice cider gets its name – juice freezing during the Swedish late autumn and winter.

Well, he achieved what he set out to – apart from the "great" bit. The natural property of these Swedish apples produced an almost unpalatably acidic cider. So Andreas decided that he had to make a naturally sweet cider to balance the acidity. He sought the assistance of Eleanor Léger of Eden Cider in Vermont to make an ice cider, with some immediately outstanding results. Through some voracious blogging, Andreas had caught the attention of the Swedish wine press, who were desperate for an indigenous drink of substance. So the release of his cider made a bit of a stir.

Now, with an orchard of his own, comprising hardy Russian, Finnish and Swedish apple varieties, Andreas has grown Brännland Cider from strength to strength, gaining listings with Michelin-starred restaurants across Europe. Bravo.

DRINK IT

ISCIDER Unctuous, nectar-like sweet fruitiness combines with velveteen viscosity and tingly acidity. Yeah, it's pretty good.

ANDREAS'S FAVOURITE APPLE

"Wow, that's hard," was Andreas's answer to this question. But if he had to name a favourite apple it would have to be the Swedish variety **INGRID MARIE**. "Ingrid Marie has a wonderful smoothness and is very much a classic apple. It also is the core of what we feel ice cider should be. A red apple that balances sugar and sweetness."

ABOVE: The end result – a product that exudes all of the confidence, charm and finesse of a wine.

AUSTRALIA

In a land full (well, not exactly full – there's still a bit of free space) of beer-swilling larrakins and fine wine degustators, it's hard to imagine cider holding much of a place in the national drinking psyche. Well, the truth is that it has a unique and ever-growingly influential role for Aussie drinkers.

A ustralia is the fourth-largest cider-consuming nation on the planet, quaffing some 166 million litres (43.9 million gallons) in 2016, but it is also one of the fastest growing markets, expanding to accommodate the different styles being produced and the occasions being found to consume them.

Without wishing to make bold, generalized, stereotypical statements, Australia can get hot. Very hot. So hot it can melt a dingo. So hot… you get my drift. Thirst-quenching drinks do pretty well, hence the popularity of beer. But not everyone likes beer, and quaffing a few (exquisite) Margaret River Chardonnays to hit the spot is quite probably ill-advised. Enter cold cider with its crisp acidity, slaking thirsts left, right and centre. Job done.

Flavoured ciders are a big thing, especially for the young, but also on the march, from a much smaller base, are ciders that take a lead from wine. On the mainland (Tasmania is a law unto itself), apples tend to be grown in the same sort of sheltered pockets that vines inhabit, so maybe it should come as no surprise that wine makers are experimenting with producing some truly awesome ciders.

BELOW: Y-shaped apple-tree growing at Willie Smith's orchards in Tasmania. This tree shape is used to increase light levels and air flow.

RECOMMENDED AUSTRALIAN CIDERS

NORMAN CIDER
LOBO Cider

PEAR CIDER
The Hills Cider Company

PINK LADY CIDER
The Apple Thief

MC CIDER
Flying Brick Cider Co.

23 VARIETIES
Willie Smith's

SEXUAL CONSENT
Sparkke

HOWLER
Darkes Cider

HILLBILLY SCRUMPY
Hillbilly Cider

'ARF 'N 'ARF
Daylesford Cider

NORFOLK STILL
Small Acres Cyder

HENRY OF HARCOURT

Located in the apple-growing heart of Central Victoria, this unique cidery was established by Drew and Irene Henry back in the early 1990s. Sick of not getting paid enough by the supermarkets for their dessert apples, Drew planted up a huge array of English and French cider apples and perry pears and chanced his arm at making some artisan cider under the name of Henry of Harcourt.

ABOVE AND RIGHT: Unique ciders made from English and French apples, planted over twenty years ago.

The name evokes the image of a Knight of the Realm, murderous yet emotionally complex – as if he were Sir Lancelot's nefarious drinking buddy, the guy who was actually quite empathetic and enjoyed painting watercolours.

Anyway, back to reality. The amazing thing about Drew was that he was planting these apple and pear varieties over 20 years ago, way before the renaissance of cider and without any kind of support network. In order to succeed, he had to call upon all the guile, skill and redoubtable can-do attitude of someone who had worked as a mining geologist for 40 years in countries such as Papua New Guinea, Indonesia, West Africa and Russia. And succeed he did, for the wares from Henry of Harcourt are some of the most wonderful, idiosyncratic ciders you've ever tasted.

Why do I call them idiosyncratic? Well, at first it's a little challenging to get your head round having Dabinett, Yarlington Mill and Co. growing in a landscape where the biggest pests are grazing grey kangaroos rather than mildew. It's as if badgers in

The Shire suddenly got a taste for cider apples and were able to climb the trees, seeking out the sugary goodness. Madness.

It's the supreme growing conditions that make this place special. Long, hot, dry summers flow into warm, dry autumns. The resultant high sugars in the apples ensure that a high alcohol can be achieved, with the Dabinett hitting 10 percent ABV. Holy moly! But these ciders have been made with such skill, care and precision that, despite being bone dry and highly palate-warming, they display all the finesse and elegance of a wine but, critically, still retain their varietal characters.

Sadly, Drew passed away in 2017, but his legacy of uncompromising and award-winning cider making continues with son Michael, their chief cider maker, at the helm, ably supported by his partner Troy, their pommelier, and by head orchardist, Irene. In their words, the orchard and the farm don't stop, even for the most profound events. As a family, they feel beholden to the land and to their community, but more than that, they feel compelled to continue what has been a 20-year journey. We should all wish them every success for the future.

DRINK IT
KINGSTON BLACK The king of cider apples gets an antipodean twist, tipping the scales at over 11 percent ABV. This is a seriously big cider, the equivalent of a ballsy Semillon or swaggering Chablis grand cru. Liquorice and stone fruits on the nose give way to bold tannins, fresh acidity and no small amount of fruitiness. Wowzers.

HENRY OF HARCOURT'S FAVOURITE APPLE
KINGSTON BLACK.

RIGHT: Drew Henry – Australian cider pioneer, bastion of quality and general legend. He will be sorely missed.

NEW ZEALAND

The Land of the Long White Cloud has been increasing its reputation for quality drinks production for decades, and in Marlborough Sauvignon Blanc it has one of the iconic global wine brands. Latterly, demand for funky and pungent NZ hop varieties, such as Nelson Sauvin and Motueka, and the associated indigenous brews, has sky-rocketed with the global craft beer boom. Now attention has turned toward cider and, given that New Zealand is a large exporter of eating apples, such as Pink Lady, Granny Smith and Smitten, it is not short of quality, high-acid fruit.

C ider volumes have increased pretty rapidly in New Zealand over the last decade, with the majority coming by way of offerings from the larger brewers. To be fair, some are making a pretty good effort of producing a mainstream cider on a large scale. But some ciders (made by bigger and smaller producers) are woefully lacking some skill and are majorly faulty. Thankfully, there are some truly creative, bold and innovative ciders coming out of NZ. You can sense that the cider market is at a similar stage to where craft beer was ten years ago.

A pessimist might say that NZ cider has an identity crisis – it has no established style and consumers are still broadly unaware of the cider opportunity. On the other hand, you could say that it stands on the verge of a revolution. The consumer is just starting to become aware of the varied wonders of the fermented apple which, using the great raw materials grown there, expert fermenting skill and some good old Kiwi ingenuity, can create some truly great drinks.

Now is the time for cider makers and drinkers to coalesce, and through the sharing of knowledge, experimentation and judicious quality control, start the journey to cider nirvana.

THE CIDEROLOGIST'S
RECOMMENDED NEW ZEALAND CIDERS & PERRIES

NEWTOWN PIPPIN
Zeffer Cider Co.

PERFECT PEAR
The Cider Factorie

FINE ABOUT THE RANGES
Forecast Cider

MAYFLOWER
Edgebrook Cider

SCENIC RESERVE
Three Wise Birds

PILGRIM'S DRY
Paynter's Hawke's
Bay Cider

MÉTHODE CIDER
Abel

**EVIL GENIUS
IMPERIAL CIDER**
Scoundrels and Rogues

PECKHAM'S CIDERY & ORCHARD

I have to confess that I have an ulterior motive for shining a spotlight onto Peckham's, based in the Nelson region, at the top of South Island. It was the complete stab in the dark on the part of Alex and Caroline Peckham that enabled me to move to New Zealand back in 2013. They were willing to take a punt on a guy from the UK on the basis of a few emails and telephone calls, and employed me as an assistant cider maker. Not only that, but I lived on their farm for a while and, even after moving to a new property (a whole 70m/77 yards away), continued to use sofas and chairs previously stashed in their garage.

Their generosity enabled me to undertake this ludicrous cider journey. So, yeah, I like these guys. But it just so happens that they are also currently the best cider makers in New Zealand. And you don't have to take my word for it – they have been crowned national champions for three years in a row.

So how and why are these guys the best? Well, a large chunk is down to Alex and Caroline themselves, and their dedication to never cutting corners, even when that is to their financial detriment, and to making the best drinks that they can.

The land plays its part, too. The Moutere Valley, where Peckham's Cidery & Orchard is located, is a growing area of significant repute. Apples, pears, grapes, hops, boysenberries and blackcurrants all abound in this super-growing micro-climate. Sunny Nelson, indeed.

ABOVE: One of the superstars of New Zealand cider, Home Block is a blend of the best from the cider-apple orchards on the farm.

LEFT: Caroline Peckham, one half of multi-award-winning Peckham's Cider duo.

Inspired by the ciders they drank in their native England when they were younger, when Alex and Caroline settled on an apple farm in the Moutere valley, they grafted the vast majority of the existing dessert-apple trees over to traditional West Country cider apples. They sourced these varieties by scouring pretty much the entirety of the country over a couple of years. Now with many acres of new plantings of varieties such as Knotted Kernel, Kingston Black, Tom Putt and Major, they boast the largest West Country cider-apple orchard in the country.

The Peckhams put these varieties to the test through their innovative cider-making endeavours to create an incredible range – flavoured with feijoa (it's a fruit – you'll know if you've been to NZ), wild-fermented, hopped, ice cider and keeved (*see* page 91) to name but a few. Whatever style or new blend they attempt, they just seem to get it right every time. I like to think at least a bit of this skill was down to some of the influence I brought when I worked here. It isn't. They're just extraordinarily good and dedicated.

ABOVE, TOP: Alex Peckham, among a young block of English cider apple trees on the home farm in Upper Moutere, Nelson.

ABOVE, BOTTOM: Ex-chardonnay barrels from the world-renowned Neudorf winery across the road add texture and complexity to maturing ciders.

DRINK IT

HOME BLOCK An annual blend of the best aged, small-batch fermentations of bittersweet and bittersharp ciders. Appley, earthy and tart. Off-dry. Awesome.

ALEX & CAROLINE'S FAVOURITE APPLE
KNOTTED KERNEL.

SOUTH AFRICA

Rather amazingly, South Africa is the second-largest cider-consuming nation on the planet, after the UK, and is home to two of the world's top five ciders by volume. Much like its southern hemisphere counterparts in Australia and New Zealand, with a strong apple-export industry and famed wine making culture, it should maybe come as no surprise that it makes significant quantities of cider. But because there is only one South African brand – Savanna – that has any decent export volume, the world isn't always aware that South Africa is a proud cider-producing nation.

Back in 2000, H P Bulmer Ltd (then still a family-owned company) attempted to enter into the domestic South African market, eyeing up the way consumption was increasing. Alas, as with its ill-fated ventures in China and the USA, this international expansion was a cause of the downfall of the world's largest cider maker and its eventual sale.

South African's proclivity for drinking cider continues today: it is currently the second-fastest growing market in the world. This growth is partly driven by improved distribution and awareness, but also by the range of ciders now available. It's true that the considerable majority of this volume comes from one single mega-producer – Distell – but there are some young upstarts too.

RIGHT: South African cider is dominated by one big player, but there are some smaller, crafty upstarts emerging.

SXOLLIE

Back in 2014, a group of Cape Town-based entrepreneurs attempted to stick it to the man by bringing a small-batch, 100-percent juice cider onto the market. Establishing a small, progressive cider business in South Africa is tough, apparently – licence delays, no access to credit, an over-bureaucratic tax regime and lifeless, small-scale distribution. In the face of these challenges, Sxollie was born.

ABOVE: Exuding all the cool, indie attitude of craft beer, Sxollie is tapping into a new generation's thirst for something different.

Pronounced *sko-llie*, and derived from the English word "scallywag", Sxollie is a colloquial term for a hustler or cheeky renegade – a name that perfectly embodies the company's counter-corporate attitude. This is an urban brand for an urban consumer, but still very much retaining its African roots.

Despite exuding the craft beer aesthetic and attitude with bold, contemporary design and language, the Sxollie range puts the fruit centre stage. Using apples and pears sourced in the Elgin Valley, close to Cape Town, these drinks are a pure expression of the chosen varieties – just like the local wines.

Sxollie produces three different single-varietal products – Gala, Granny Smith and Packham Pear. I like the fact that they halt the fermentation to ensure that a natural, residual sweetness is retained. They won't be everyone's cup of ~~tea~~ cider, but for me they are a brilliant way of engaging with a younger, urban consumer who may never have considered cider before.

DRINK IT
PACKHAM PEAR PERRY Creaminess and honey from the natural sugars balance with neat acidity and a touch of stone-fruit grippiness to give an entirely satisfying drink.

SXOLLIE'S FAVOURITE APPLE
Producing ciders in a wine style, Sxollie takes pleasure in likening its apples to grapes. During the endless days of South African summer there is no crisper, cleaner or more refreshing wine than a Sauvignon Blanc, and to that would equate the **GRANNY SMITH**. Tart, zingy and citrusy, a cold Granny Smith apple always hits the spot.

SOUTH AMERICA

Apples are grown, and modest amounts of cider made, across the temperate areas of South America – notably Argentina and Chile. These apples would have been brought over by Spanish settlers several hundreds of years ago. There is also a theory that the presence of some of the apples, and the resultant cider, on this continent is a result of Welsh migrants coming to Argentina in the 19th century and creating settlements in the Patagonia region, south of Buenos Aires.

In South America, *sidra* is classically known as a sweet, sparkling drink, served almost exclusively around the holiday season, as a Christmas or New Year's eve toast. Many see it as a novelty, drunk tokenistically because it is "the thing to do" during this period. Because South American wines and beers are so good, *sidra* is often viewed as being of comparatively poor quality.

In Chile there is a rustic, rural, fermented apple drink called *chicha* – something akin to a UK scrumpy. Again, it is not highly thought of beyond the confines of rural tradition and is generally considered an old-fashioned drink.

However, as we can see across the globe, the craft beer boom and the continued interest in different styles of wine are ensuring that cider generates some interest with younger people. Some ciders are being packaged in 330-ml (12-oz) bottles with crown caps and contemporary branding – appealing to this younger generation. Other producers are utilizing the *charmat*, or even the full *méthode traditionnelle*, processes to create sparkling ciders that are bold and complex and pair well with food.

Most of the fruit used for making *sidra* in South America is sourced from modern, commercial apple orchards, with commonly grown dessert varieties. There is, however, a long-standing heritage of growing apples in these temperate regions, and it these "heritage" varieties that are proving of interest to the new wave of cider producers, owing to the structure, boldness and complexity they afford.

ABOVE: The apple-growing, and also cider-making, culture in South America is linked to the Spanish settlers.

QUEBRADA DEL CHUCAO

In the Tolten Valley, at the heart of Chile's southern Araucanía region, two cousins are taking the old tradition of making apple *chicha* very much into the 21st century. This tradition, which dates back to the colonial era, interested Diego Rivera so much that, while studying oenology, he did his thesis on Chilean cider. When Matías Nahrwold joined him in 2012, Quebrada del Chucao was born.

The company sources fruit from a number of local orchards with old varieties that carry local names such as Alvarado and Roja Chica. These low-yielding trees produce fruit with intensity of flavour and sugar, enabling the cousins to come up with bold, dry ciders.

Diego and Matías are also conducting research into precisely what these old-fashioned varieties are, so that cuttings can be taken from them to graft new specimens, to ensure these apples continue to exist for future generations.

DRINK IT:

SIDRA ESPUMANTE Made by the *méthode traditionnelle* and exquisitely presented, this cider pours a bright golden colour. The natural, crisp acidity and acute dryness are cleverly tempered with soft, brioche characters developed through the lees aging process.

ABOVE AND RIGHT: Wine-making knowledge is being applied to cider making in southern Chile, resulting in exquisitely tasty cider.

FAVOURITE APPLE
ROJA CHICA.

WASSAIL!

If you happen to be in the West of England during January, you might catch sight and sound of some rather unexpected activities. Some rather pagan activities. For one month a year, an area famed for its tranquility and gentle nature packs away the tea and cucumber sandwiches and reaches instead for the shotguns and flaming torches.

assailing is one of those wonderful British traditions that has just about managed to hang on into the 21st century. Despite modern health and safety regulations, it sits alongside cheese-rolling, shin-kicking, bog-snorkelling and burning-barrel racing as a relic of a bygone age. But in these digitally disparate, hyper-connected, lightning-speed times, there is something exceedingly comforting about gadding about in a muddy orchard in the freezing cold, participating in an event that has old, old roots.

Still critical to the cider-making calendar of the UK, wassail is celebrated on Twelfth Night, the pagan New Year's Eve, commonly held to be 6 January. In the deepest and darkest parts of the cider world, though, it happens on 17 January, also known as "Old Twelvey" – the *true* pagan New Year. Twelfth Night has only been celebrated on 6 January since 1752, when Britain controversially moved over to the Gregorian calendar, sparking riots among those who objected to the apparent loss of 11 days.

The term "wassail" can trace its origins to pre-Christian Britain. Anglo-Saxon tradition included a New Year celebration in the halls of the Lord of the Manor, including a mighty feast with a giant bowl of a sort of punch: a mix of cider, ale and mead infused with bountiful

ABOVE: Wassailing is an ancient tradition with pagan roots.

spices and crab apples. The Lord would toast those present with the cry of *waes hael*, meaning "be whole" or "good health", and the hearty response would be *drink hael* (I think you can guess what that means).

The idea of wassailing – blessing, toasting, sharing and giving thanks during the Yuletide period – has continued through the centuries.

Wassailing is one of those wonderful British traditions that has just about managed to hang on into the 21st century.

The Victorians seized on its spirit of generosity by endorsing the concept of wassailing from door to door – poorer folk singing songs in return for charitable gifts, rather than begging. This soon morphed into the ever-popular Christmas carolling. And, of course, the much enjoyed winter warmer, mulled cider (often known as *wassail* and a far more palatable spiced drink than its vinous cousin, IMHO), is a direct descendent of the original spiced cider punch drunk all those centuries back.

But it's in the orchard that the wassail has really retained its significance and mythical status. The earliest accounts of wassailing fruit trees come from the East of England – in St Albans in 1486 and Kent in 1585. But it isn't until the 17th and 18th centuries that the wassail truly comes to prominence.

Every region, village and farm would have had its own version of the ceremony, with unique traditions, symbols and rituals. Wassails from the Welsh Marches (the border country between England and Wales) may be quite different from those further southwest. But generally speaking the event begins with a torch-lit procession around the cider

orchard, with revellers crashing pots and pans to scare off insidious forces, often led by a Wassail King and Queen (think Pearly Kings and Queens but with more vegetative adornments and West Country accents). The Master of Ceremony, a figure regaled in black, is called the Butler, and he or she calls the congregation to gather around the largest tree in the orchard, which has 12 small bonfires placed around it, representing the 12 zodiac signs or 12 apostles. In Herefordshire, there is a 13th bonfire within the circle, which upon lighting is promptly extinguished underfoot. The reason? It is known as the Judas Fire and shalt not be allowed to burn its treacherous flame (or something like that!).

The Butler leads the crowd in singing songs appealing to Pomona, the apple

ABOVE: At the heart of wassailing are people and community – this is a time and place for sharing and thanks. And druids with megaphones.

OPPOSITE: Crucial to the wassail is the torchlight procession through the orchard, blowing horns and crashing pans to scare away the evil spirits.

goddess, for a healthy harvest. The smallest boy in the crowd, known as the Tom Tit, is then hoisted up high and places cider-soaked bread into the branches of the apple tree – a signifier of good luck. Just to make sure that any malevolent forces have been fully banished, shotguns are fired to rid these lands of them. And finally, a bowl of cider is passed around from person to person, with "wassail" being proffered and "drinkhail"

offered in return: "good health" and "cheers". It's basically *The Wicker Man*, but with cider.

The one common denominator of these myriad customs, however, and the true spirit of wassail, is the opportunity for everyone in the community to get together and to give thanks, to share and celebrate these traditions that are such a key part of the landscapes and cultures of cider making regions. In these fast-paced times, it's great to slow down a bit with a night out in the orchards, singing the songs of generations before and harking back to a simpler age. Although the cider is probably tastier these days.

The Campaign for the Revival Of Wassailing (CROW) is a group of professional miscreants from Gloucestershire who are passionate about this tradition. These folk eloquently describe why the wassail is the tonic for our times:

It creates an atmosphere where we can make amends, end hostilities, forgive insults, heal wounds and let bygones be bygones. It creates an atmosphere where we can make new friends, especially between the old and young and between the sexes. It creates a better working relationship and feelings of unity, of all being as one. I'll toast to that. Pomona knows, the world could do with a little more of this right now.

GLOBAL WASSAIL

Although the wassail is essentially an English tradition, as the popularity of cider grows, so does the interest in interpreting these old customs in new parts of the world.

In Tasmania, Australia, award-winning cider maker Willie Smith's hosts a huge, annual midwinter festival, full of pagan goodness and with a West Country-inspired wassail at the heart of the event.

Back in 2014, a small settlement at the top of New Zealand's South Island saw its very own wassail, led by yours truly. We lived in a home with modest insulation, a wood burner, an electric heater and no central heating. In NZ that's called a warm house. In the cosmopolitan metropolis of Neudorf Road,

Upper Moutere (population 13 – and a few pukekos), you need to find ways to entertain yourself when it's cold and dark.

This is especially important as Christmas is in the height of summer in the southern hemisphere, meaning there is no midwinter celebration. Now, being a self-respecting British man, there was no way I was going to go a whole winter without creating some spurious reason to eat bowel-bloatingly enormous portions of food and consume an ill-advised quantity of booze. Therefore, along with our European friends and their friends, we decided to stage our own Christmas/ wassail/midwinter solstice/pagan celebration. And have flaming torches.

So, it came to pass that on a frosty 21 June, a multi-national contingent (three Brits, two Germans, one Swiss-Belgian, one French guy and a Japanese dude) descended on Upper Moutere to wassail the night away. The group included two cheese-makers, a wine maker, a brewer and a former cider maker. So you could say that we ate and drank well. In fact (hyperbole alert), we think there was no group of people in the whole of New Zealand

ABOVE: The Morris men often lead the procession and rouse the crowd into song: "Oh apple tree, we wassail thee…"

OPPOSITE: An old English mythical character, replete in classic attire. And the Spirit of the Green Man.

that evening consuming such locally sourced, fresh and tasty produce. It was lush.

We lit the flaming torches and headed into the paddock next to our house to seek out the little apple trees tucked in the corner. We sang to the trees, placed cider-soaked bread onto the branches and shared cider from the hand-carved wassail bowl that had been shipped over from the UK. Was this the first wassail ever in NZ? I reckon so, but even if it wasn't, it was pretty good fun.

As a perfect reflection of the intertwining cultures that this area of NZ seems to cultivate, Yas, the Japanese guy, made up and played a song on his traditional, hand-made Moroccan sintir about this old, English tradition. It was simply called "Wassssssssaaaaayyyyooooooo". Amazing.

10

PERRY:
THE FORGOTTEN DRINK

Perry is the unheralded, and certainly less consumed, cousin of cider. In many ways (and I'll say this quietly), perry is more important to me. It's not necessarily that I prefer drinking it to cider – that is more a question of occasion – it's simply that the tradition of making perry in the UK is unique to the region I am from. Perry truly is our indigenous wine, for it can display all the florality, freshness and lightness of touch of any aromatic white wine.

Today, only a relatively small quantity of perry is made in the traditional heartlands of the English/Welsh borders, the Domfront region of France, and the Central European belt of Luxembourg, Switzerland and Austria, but it has a long history. As far back at the 4th century, the Roman agricultural writer Palladius gave instructions on how to make a fermented pear drink, then called *castomoniale*.

The drink that has come to be produced in the UK and northern France is not made from dessert pears. Oh no. The pears that provide this luscious liquor are definitely not for eating. Once called "choke" pears on account of their palate-massacring nature, they are the bastard children of the wild *Pyrus pyraster* and the domesticated *Pyrus communis*, brought to northern Europe by the Romans.

With the fall of the Roman Empire, their well-tended gardens, containing all manner of cultivated fruits, fell into ruin and these domesticated pears were set loose on the British countryside, cross-breeding with the natives to create a whole gene pool of new varieties. These "ferals" lurked on the edges of woodlands and in hedgerows. William of Malmesbury at the start of the 12th century wrote about my county of Gloucestershire:

Here you may see the highways and common lanes clad with apple trees and pear trees not set nor grafted by the industry of man's hand, but growing naturally of their own accord.

By the 17th century, it was apparent that people had begun to understand the potentially wonderful drink that could be created through the fermentation of these otherwise unconsumable pears. Specific named varieties were being lauded for the quality of perry they produced – Taynton Squash, Hartpury Green and Huffcap, to name a few.

John Evelyn (*see* page 37), in his study of the British cider and perry industry, *Pomona*, written in 1664, noted that not even pigs could cope with the intense bitterness and astringency of the Barland variety (still in existence), spitting them out in disgust. The perry this variety produces (which I have made a few gallons of in the past) is suitably bold and jaw-grindingly chewy. Lush.

THE THREE COUNTIES

Unlike cider, which has a long-standing heritage of being made in all parts of the southern UK, traditional perry is a firmly rooted native of a specific geographical area,

that of The Three Counties of Gloucestershire, Herefordshire and Worcestershire (and if I'm feeling generous, a little bit over the border into Monmouthshire in Wales).

Pear trees grow quite differently from apple trees. Firstly in terms of shape and size, with apple trees crowning over and often being wider than they are tall. Perry pears, on the other hand, can grow into colossal giants. They can be as large and robust as an oak – 15m (50ft) tall with a 3.5-m (12-ft) trunk circumference. I truly wonder if there is another fruit tree in the world that can match the sheer mass of a large perry pear (if you know the answer, please do write in).

Their habit is to grow up toward the sky, with crotches that make them look like telegraph poles, upside-down Christmas trees or broad-spanning cathedral arches. Though, of course, there are exceptions – the variety Butt, for example, has an entirely idiosyncratic and unmistakable, weeping willow-type shape.

And then there's the age of these trees – 200, 300, maybe even 400 years old. The old adage advises you to "plant pears for your heirs", such is the sluggishness with which they grow, but also the great age they can achieve. To visit an old perry pear orchard is like venturing into a time capsule. It is an honour and a bit of a head rush to wander around orchards that were being grafted before the USA had even won its independence.

The status and importance of perry in this region should not be underestimated. In the village of Much Marcle, Herefordshire,

Perry truly is Britain's indigenous wine.

ABOVE: The battle between the rootstock and the intended variety can create dramatic graft unions, such as this "corset" shape.

lies Hellens, one of the oldest houses in Britain. You approach it via a wonderful, long undulating driveway. And what finer way to demonstrate the grandeur of the property than by planting an avenue of trees? No oaks or beeches here, though. Instead, the driveway is resplendent with perry-pear trees. And, incredibly, there are still specimens of the original plantation, which was made in 1710 to commemorate the coronation of Queen Anne.

VARIETIES

There are thought to be over 100 different perry-pear varieties in the UK – and that's only the ones that have been identified. The fruit of each and every one has its own

OPPOSITE: These perry pears come in all shapes and sizes and many have enough tannin to turn your mouth drier than the Atacama Desert.

Not even pigs could cope with the intense bitterness and astringency of the Barland variety of perry pear, spitting them out in disgust.

ABOVE: Every perry-pear variety has its own story and can be traced to a region, village, or individual farm.

unique shape: although normally of the classic *pyriform*, they can also be egg-shaped (Huffcap), squashed flat (Gin) or perfectly spherical and the size of marbles (Holmer).

There are many instances of just a single mature specimen of a particular variety existing. Without work to propagate these varieties in museum orchards (which is thankfully happening), names such as Waterlugg, Coppy and Cowslip would never be heard again.

Perry pears have an array of names. Some are eponymous to their village of origin, such as Dymock Red. Some are named after individual farms, such as Oldfield. On occasion, prominent people have had pears dedicated to them, such as Judge Amphlett, a respected Worcestershire Assizes judge from the early 20th century. And sometimes a variety's impact on the constitution can be so great that its informs the name. The diuretic effects of one pear are so powerful that it has been named Startlecock!

Compared to cider, perry is a lighter and more delicate drink, but each of these varieties has different flavour and aroma characteristics: from zingy grapefruit to luscious watermelon, and earthy robustness to perfumed elderflower, perries made from these pears can be the most refined and fabulous that can be tasted.

PERRY-PEAR HUNTERS

Perry pears incite a fervour, an insatiable quest, among certain people. Until 30 years ago, the majority of knowledge and understanding of these ancient varieties was lost. The considerable amount that we know today is largely down to Charles Martell, best known for his Stinking Bishop Cheese. With detective skills that *CSI* would be proud of, and a dogged determination, Charles has almost singlehandedly positively identified a huge number of varieties that were previously thought lost.

I was privileged to accompany him to an orchard in Dymock where he had an inkling that another "thought lost" variety was lurking. We convened one autumnal afternoon, several years back. Charles was armed with no more than a recollection of a conversation from 20 years previously; I came with nothing more useful than a packed lunch (cheese and onion sandwiches and a scotch

BELOW: Picking pears can be an onerous task – they mature from the inside out, so it can be challenging to know when they're ready.

THE CIDEROLOGIST'S
FIVE FAVOURITE PERRY PEARS

THORN
Wonderfully brisk, zesty and grapefruity. This is a great breakfast perry!

WINNAL'S LONGDON
I don't know who Winnal was, but they have a brilliantly balanced pear named after them.

BUTT
Why? Because it produces an incredibly bold, tannic and chewy perry (and also because I'm juvenile).

GIN
Perry from this variety is acid, lean and mineral.

MOORCROFT
Known in Dymock as Stinking Bishop, the best perry I ever tasted came from this variety.

egg – classic). The odds didn't look good. Thankfully, Charles's memory is pretty good and we identified the potential tree.

The "lost" variety had, by all accounts, not produced a particularly interesting perry, and so had been chopped off the rootstock and replaced with a new variety called Turner's Barn – a process known as "head-working". Turner's Barn produces idiosyncratic, clustered, vertical branches, so it was easy to identify, along with its rather squat, auburn fruit. And there, between the rootstock and the Turner's Barn were a few branches of egg-shaped, lime-green pears – the variety

ABOVE: These pears ripen from the inside out so it can be hard to tell when they're at their optimal point for harvesting.

that had been originally grafted onto the rootstock. We had struck gold! World, meet Hampton Rough. The rediscovery of this pear has meant that cuttings have been taken for grafting onto new trees, so this variety can be safeguarded for the future.

One pear variety that has eluded the most ardent hunter is Late Treacle. Although it's not for the want of trying. Unlike most other pears, Late Treacle sports pink blossom, rather than the customary white. And so, legend has it, a particularly passionate individual chartered a plane to fly around the Gloucestershire/Herefordshire border in late April one year to try to spot the oasis of pink amid the sea of white. They were unsuccessful, and the legend of Late Treacle continues.

CONSTITUTION
As mentioned on page 114, all perry contains sorbitol, a naturally occurring unfermentable

sugar. The effect of this is to provide a pleasant, natural sweetness. But there is a downside – sorbitol is a laxative. Many a person over the centuries has had a perry and then had the urgent and uncontrollable urge to find a toilet very quickly.

The old saying goes:

Perry goes down like sunshine,
Round and round like thunder,
And comes out like lightning!

TERROIR AND PAGAN GODS
So why is it that perry historically was concentrated on such as a small geographical area? The centre of the UK perry universe is an unassuming, but entirely iconic landmark in the Gloucestershire countryside. Just a stone's throw from my beloved Dymock, May Hill sits proudly on the edge of the Severn Valley and can be seen from some 50km (30 miles) around. It is easily recognizable thanks to a stand of pine trees planted atop it in 1887 to commemorate the Golden Jubilee of Queen Victoria. The old saying goes, "If you're within sight of May Hill, you're in perry country", and this is entirely true. This may be because of the *terroir*, of which I shall speak more in a moment. But there is an alternative, slightly more pagan theory…

…After the gods had finished creating the Earth, they sat on the top of May Hill, lording over the splendour of their creation. Their slumber was interrupted by a small godling eagerly running up the hill, clutching a piece of fruit in its hand. Arriving at the top, the little godling, addressing the chief god, breathlessly exclaimed, "I have found the elixir of life!" and handed over the fruit.

The chief god grasped the fruit and took a large bite, but quickly its face gurned in

OPPOSITE: Gabe sets to work with the panking pole. He's a professional panker, you know.

horror and disgust and it spat the fruit out.

"That's not the elixir of life," the chief roared. "That's bloody horrible!"

The little godling squealed in reply, "No, you're supposed to squeeze the fruit and extract its juice, and that will give you the elixir of life."

But, of course, by now it was too late – the fruit had been spat out and the seeds had scattered across the land. And from the ground emerged magnificent pear trees.

PERRY TODAY

So why is a drink that has the potential to rival any sparkling white wine made in such small quantities today? There are a number of reasons. First, perry is hard to make. Some perry-pear varieties have a perfect window of ripeness that lasts about 17 minutes before they disintegrate into mush. Others, such as Butt, are rock-hard for months. Another old saying goes:

Gather yer Butts one year,

Mill them the next,

And drink it the year after.

Perry is also more susceptible to infection than cider. Without the bold, robust tannins and with a propensity to produce ethyl acetate (which you may remember I likened earlier to nail-varnish remover), it can often turn out fairly rank.

Perry did for a time exist as a commercial product. In the 1950s, Showerings, the cider maker from Shepton Mallet, Somerset, planted up a large perry-pear orchard and latched onto the idea of producing a cheaper, UK version of sparkling white wine. The result: Babycham. It was the first alcoholic beverage to be advertised on TV, and its marketing hinged on the use of the term "Champagne Perry". For a time, this brand was synonymous with class and elegance. Such was its popularity that Showerings' Herefordshire rival, Bulmers, produced its own perry, called Golden Godwin. The company went to some

efforts to usurp Babycham as the lady's drink of choice, even hiring blonde bombshell Diana Dors to front advertisements. However, from the late 70s onward, the brand started to lose its appeal, with the "Bambi" brand icon becoming synonymous with naffness. As with most things, the brand has somewhat come back into fashion over the last decade, not from a drinking perspective, but with the kitsch aesthetic of the saucers being the height of retro chic.

When the cider revolution came around again post-"Magners effect", and further innovations were being sought, the idea of using pears came up more. However, the word "perry" would have meant nothing to the target, younger consumer and would have had chintzy, Babycham connotations for the older one. So the name Pear Cider was adopted – much to the annoyance of some smaller producers, who thought it was anathema.

WHANAU, WHENUA, WHAKAPAPA

But my passion for this drink goes beyond the final product. Perry is entirely synonymous with and local to my region. What do I call this (other than awesome, obviously)? I call it *terroir*. There is something about the soils, underlying geology, rainfall and sunshine levels, combined with a historical penchant and appreciation for this drink, that means that these very specific pear varieties find their home within this small radius of May Hill. Which makes this my indigenous drink. It's my link to the land; my sense of place.

It's also a direct link to my family. Before I had made a drop of cider, my first foray into fermentation was 23 litres (6 gallons) of perry made from the last remaining Thorn tree on my Granny's farm. As I mentioned earlier, my Grandad, who died before I was born, had made perry from this tree, as, undoubtedly, had generations before him. The act of making that perry put me on speed-dial to my forebears and to a tradition that has continued for centuries, and I haven't stopped talking since.

When I lived in New Zealand, I discovered that the indigenous Maori people have many fundamental principles, but three key tenets: *whanau* (family and community), *whenua* (land) and *whakapapa* (ancestry). And that's it. That absolutely nails it. It's ironic, of course, that it took moving 18,500km (11,500 miles) to the other side of the world to find the words to articulate succinctly what makes perry, and my little corner of The Shire, so unique and important. Even if it does cause Startlecock.

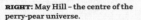

RIGHT: May Hill – the centre of the perry-pear universe.

11

CIDER & FOOD

It is fair to say that when most of us think of a drink to pair with a meal, that drink will normally be a variety of wine. And for very good reasons. The aromas, flavours and textures from the myriad types and styles of wine can complement a wealth of different foods. Does anything go better with seafood than a Sauvignon Blanc, or can the richness of a steak be enhanced more than by a fine Malbec? The opportunities are endless.

It's important to remember that there are no rules. If you think a cider goes with a particular food, and enhances your enjoyment of the food, then go for it.

The might of the global beer industry has put considerable effort (and expense) into introducing consumers to the concept of matching beers with food. But at the risk of incurring the wrath of my hop- and malt-inclined friends, and the wider beer fraternity, I am of the opinion that beer can't complement food as well as wine does.

Cider, on the other hand, shares all the requisite sensory qualities of wine – so much so that it can act as a more than able substitute and, for me, is often a better match. Yes, there is the stereotype of a classic farmhouse cider being drunk with hearty slabs of bread and cheese, but the matching potential of cider goes way beyond this. The approach to matching cider with food is the same as it is with all drinks. First, it's important to remember that there are no rules. If you think a cider goes with a particular food, and enhances your enjoyment of the food, then go for it. Everyone has a different palate and different flavour preferences, which makes matching quite subjective. The trick is finding the right balance between the sweetness, tannin and acidity of the cider and the properties of the food. Use the chart on the following page for some perfect food-matching suggestions.

THE THREE Cs

If you do want some guidance on how to approach this brave new world and save your taste buds from a potentially challenging assault, here are three guiding principles to a successful match:

CUT

Use dry, crisp and/or tannic ciders to cut through rich foods and cleanse the palate.

FOR EXAMPLE: match them with Thai fishcakes, ripe Brie or fatty lamb.

CONTRAST

Use ciders that differ in flavour and mouthfeel from the food to create balance.

FOR EXAMPLE: an intense sweet cider with a salty blue cheese, or a fruity, tannic cider with a fresh, aromatic stir-fry.

COMPLEMENT

Use ciders that accentuate similar flavours or that match the strength or delicacy of the food.

FOR EXAMPLE: a light, acid cider with white fish, a bold, tannic cider with beef bourguignon, a sweet and zingy cider with a sweet dessert such as trifle.

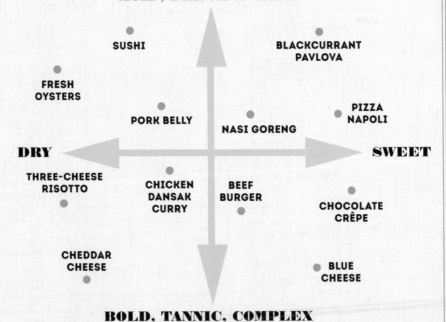

ACID, FRESH & CRISP

SUSHI

BLACKCURRANT PAVLOVA

FRESH OYSTERS

PORK BELLY

NASI GORENG

PIZZA NAPOLI

DRY

SWEET

THREE-CHEESE RISOTTO

CHICKEN DANSAK CURRY

BEEF BURGER

CHOCOLATE CRÊPE

CHEDDAR CHEESE

BLUE CHEESE

BOLD, TANNIC, COMPLEX

CIDER RECIPES

Cider is, of course, not only a wonderful accompaniment to a meal, but can be a vital ingredient also. Here are three fabulous recipes where cider steals the show.

CIDER & PORK WITH PAPPARDELLE

Serves 4

Preparation time 8 minutes

Cooking time 20 minutes

15g (½oz) dried wild mushrooms

3 tablespoons olive oil

400g (13oz) boneless pork loin steaks

150g (5oz) smoked bacon, sliced

8 shallots, quartered

300ml (½pint) dry cider

125ml (4fl oz) cider vinegar

2 thyme sprigs

1 bay leaf, torn

400g (13oz) fresh pappardelle or thick ribbon pasta

200ml (7fl oz) crème fraîche

salt and pepper

- Soak the dried mushrooms for 5–10 minutes in 6 tablespoons boiling water.

- Meanwhile, heat the oil in a large frying pan over a medium heat and fry the pork and bacon for approximately 3 minutes until browned. Add the shallots and continue frying for a further 2–3 minutes until the shallots are golden and beginning to soften.

- Pour in the dry cider and cider vinegar and add the mushrooms and soaking liquid. Stir in the herbs and season well. Bring to the boil, then reduce the heat, cover and leave to bubble gently for 10–12 minutes until the shallots are soft.

- Meanwhile, cook the pasta in a large saucepan of lightly salted boiling water for 3 minutes or according to the instructions on the packet. Drain and transfer to serving dishes.

- Stir the crème fraîche into the pork, increase the heat briefly and then place the meat on the pasta and spoon over the sauce. Serve immediately.

CIDERED CHICKEN PUFF PIE

Serves 4

Preparation time 40 minutes

Cooking time 1 hour 20 minutes

8 chicken thighs

300ml (½pint) dry cider

300ml (½pint) chicken stock

2 small leeks, slit, rinsed and sliced

50g (2oz) butter

50g (2oz) plain flour

1 tablespoon chopped tarragon

2 tablespoons chopped parsley

500g (1lb) puff pastry

flour, for dusting

1 egg, beaten, to glaze

salt and pepper

- Preheat the oven to 200°C (400°F), Gas Mark 6.

- Pack the chicken thighs into a saucepan, pour over the cider and stock, then season. Cover and simmer for 45 minutes.

- Lift the chicken out on to a plate, then add the leeks to the stock and simmer for 4–5 minutes. Strain, reserving the stock in a measuring jug. Make up the stock to 600ml (1pint) with water, if needed.

- Wash and dry the pan, then melt the butter in it. Stir in the flour, then gradually whisk in the stock and bring to the boil, stirring until the sauce is thickened. Mix in the herbs and season.

- Dice the cooked chicken, discarding the skin and bones. Put into a 1.2-litre (2-pint) pie dish with the leeks. Pour over the sauce.

- Roll out the pastry on a lightly floured surface until a little larger than the top of the pie dish. Cut 4 strips about 1cm (½inch) wide and stick along the rim with a little egg. Brush the top of the strip with egg, then press the pastry lid in place. Trim off the excess and crimp the edge. Cut leaf shapes from the excess and use to decorate the top of the pie.

- Glaze the pastry lid with egg and bake for 30 minutes or until golden.

CIDERED APPLE JELLIES

Serves 6
Preparation time 20 minutes,
plus chilling
Cooking time 15 minutes
Finishing time 5 minutes

1kg (2lb) cooking apples, peeled,
cored and sliced

300ml (½pint) cider

150ml (¼pint) water, plus 4
tablespoons

75g (3oz) caster sugar

finely grated rind of 2 lemons

4 teaspoons powdered gelatine

150ml (¼pint) double cream

- Put the apples, cider, 150ml (¼pint) of water, sugar and the rind of one of the lemons into a saucepan. Cover and simmer for 15 minutes or until the apples are soft.

- Meanwhile, put the remaining water into a small bowl and sprinkle over the gelatine, making sure that all the powder is absorbed by the water. Set aside.

- Add the gelatine to the hot apples and stir until completely dissolved. Purée the apple mixture in a blender or food processor until smooth, then pour into 6 tea cups. Allow to cool, then chill for 4–5 hours until fully set.

- When ready to serve, whip the cream until it forms soft peaks. Spoon over the jellies and sprinkle with the remaining lemon rind.

INDEX

REFERENCES

BAKER, K (Global Data). *Consumer Trends in the Global Cider Market*. 2017. Presentation produced on behalf of Global Data.

BEALE, DR J. *Aphorisms on Cider*. 1664. An essay contained within *Pomona*.

BRUNING, T. *Golden Fire: The Story of Cider*. 2012. Bright Pen Publishing.

BULMER, E.F. *Early Days of Cider Making*. 1980. Museum of Cider, Hereford. Facsimile reprint of 1937 edition.

CHAPMAN, J. *The Cider Industry and the Glass Bottle*. 2012. Society for Industrial Archaeology Journal.

CORNILLE, A., GIRAUD, T., SMULDERS, M. J., ROLDAN-RUIZ, I. & GLADIEUX, P. *The domestication and evolutionary ecology of apples*. 2014. Trends Genet. 30, 57–65.

CORNILLE, A. ET AL. *New insight into the history of domesticated apple: secondary contribution of the European wild apple to the genome of cultivated varieties*. 2012. PLoS Genet. 8:5

CROWDEN, J. 2008. *Ciderland*. Birlinn Publishing.

EVELYN, J. *Pomona* (an appendix to *Sylva*). 1664. Printed by John Martyn for the Royal Society.

GARDNER, R.J. *The Grafter's Handbook*. 2013. Revised and updated edition. Chelsea Green Publishing.

H WESTON & SONS. *Westons Cider Report 2017*. 2017. Downloaded from www.westons-cider.co.uk.

H WESTONS & SONS. *Westons Cider Report 2017 Winter Update*. 2017. Downloaded from www. westons-cider.co.uk.

JUNIPER, B.E. & MABBERLEY, D.J. *The Story of the Apple*. 2006. Timber Press

LEA, A. *Craft Cider Making*. 2015. 3rd Revised Edition. The Crowood Press.

MORGAN, J. & RICHARDS, A. *The New Book of Apples: The Definitive Guide to Over 2,000 Varieties*. 2002. Ebury Press.

NATURAL ENGLAND. *Economic, biodiversity, resource protection and social values of orchards: A study of six orchards by the Herefordshire Orchards Community Evaluation Project*. 2012. Commissioned Report NECR090.

INFORMATION & LINKS

The Beer & Cider Academy
www.beerandcideracademy.org

The Big Apple Association
www.bigapple.org.uk

Cider Australia
www.cideraustralia.org.au

Cider New Zealand
www.cidernz.com

The Ciderologist
www.theciderologist.com

Franklin County CiderDays
www.ciderdays.org

Huon Valley Mid-Winter Fest, Tasmania
www.huonvalleymidwinterfest.com.au

The New Zealand Cider Festival
www.nzciderfestival.com

Royal Bath & West Show
www.bathandwest.com/royal-bath-and-west-show/whats-on/british-cider-championships

South West of England Cidermakers' Association
www.sweca.org.uk

The Three Counties Cider & Perry Association
www.thethreecountiesciderandperryassociation.co.uk

United States Association of Cider Makers
www.ciderassociation.org

The Welsh Perry & Cider Society
www.welshcider.co.uk

GLOSSARY

ACETIC ACID The enemy of all cider makers! If air is allowed to come into contact with the cider over a prolonged period, acetic acid bacteria will start to convert alcohol into acetic acid, aka vinegar. Not good.

ACIDITY One of the key components of ciders. This is the fresh, crisp, zingy sensation, detected at the front and the sides of the mouth.

ASTRINGENCY Sensation of mouth drying/ puckering as a result of tannins from traditional West Country cider fruit. Can range from soft and gentle to full and challenging.

BITTERNESS The second sensation provided by tannins. This can again range from soft and spicy to harsh and challenging.

BLENDING The cider maker's dark art! Taking place post-fermentation, this is where cider makers use their palate to create a well-balanced cider by blending together different batches, and sweetness, if necessary.

BOTTLE-CONDITIONING The process of creating a naturally sparkling product and preserving the cider by undertaking a secondary fermentation in the bottle. The first stage of the *méthode traditionnelle*.

BOTTLE-FERMENTING The process of creating a naturally sparkling product and preserving the cider by finishing the primary fermentation in the bottle, often retaining a natural sweetness, too (*see* Keeving).

BRETTANOMYCES Also known as bret, a yeast hated by wine makers, but in small concentrations it is an important contributor to the complexity and depth of English and, especially, French ciders.

CARBON DIOXIDE Natural by-product of the fermentation process and what gives cider its fizz.

ETHYL ACETATE A cider fault produced naturally during fermentation, but present in high doses when there is poor hygiene in the cider making process. Contributes a flavour/aroma of nail-varnish remover.

FERMENTATION The magical process of natural fruit sugars being converted into alcohol and carbon dioxide through the action of yeasts. Depending on the style of cider, this process may take weeks or months.

FILTRATION Clarifying cider by forcing it across a membrane. Sterile filtration is also a process for stabilizing cider ready to go into pack.

GRAFTING Taking a cutting from the desired apple variety and physically attaching it to a sapling or tree already rooted in the ground, in order to pass on genetic material from a specific apple variety. (If you simply plant the seed, a different variety will materialize.) Apple-growers have been using this technique for thousands of years.

HARVESTING Collecting apples when they are fully ripe, ready to be milled and pressed. This can be done by hand or mechanically.

ICE CIDER A form of cider akin to a dessert wine, but produced through the fermentation of highly concentrated, sugar-rich juice. This beverage is achieved either by thawing frozen juice or by pressing frozen apples, as is the tradition in North America.

JERSEY The name given to the shape of many cider-apple varieties. Jersey types are characterized by broad shoulders, tapering to the base. They contain high quantities of tannin, creating bitter and astringent ciders.

KEEVING A traditional cider making method, now primarily used in France. Yeasts and nutrients combine in the freshly pressed juice and float to the surface to form a big, brown, cow-pat like blob, called the *chapeau brun* (brown hat). Sounds nice, right? The brilliantly clear juice, devoid of yeasts and nutrients, is removed and then undergoes a slow and incomplete fermentation, producing naturally sweet and lower-alcohol cider.

LACTIC ACID BACTERIA The predominant family of micro-flora that creates volatile phenolic aromatics in cider made from high-tannin apples, such as haybarn, clove and medicinal.

MALOLACTIC FERMENTATION A spontaneous, non-alcoholic fermentation that isn't easily controlled and is not always welcome. Can produce sour acid and diacetyl (butterscotch) flavours, which can be pleasant in the right quantities, but overpowering if they dominate.

MATURATION The post-fermentation period, lasting anything from a few weeks to a few years, whereby cider undergoes microbiological and chemical processes that produce a softer, rounder, more pleasurable drink.

MÉTHODE TRADITIONNELLE Also known as the Champagne method. In this method, cider undergoes a secondary in-bottle fermentation (*see* Bottle-conditioning) before being disgorged. Yeast is thus removed from the bottle, but the drink retains a natural sparkle.

MILL Also known as a scratter, a machine that chops apples into a pulp ready to be pressed.

ORCHARD Where we get our lovely apples from, defined as an intentional planting of five or more apple trees in a land parcel. Old traditional orchards are known as standard orchards; modern orchards are called bush orchards.

PANKING POLE A highly technical piece of orcharding equipment. It consists of a long pole with a crook and a spike. It is traditionally used to shake the branches of large apple trees in order to get the fruit down to the ground for picking.

PEAR CIDER The result of fermenting culinary pear juice. A term invented in the last 15 years and applied to modern, mainstream products.

PERRY The traditional, old drink from The Three Counties of Gloucestershire, Herefordshire and Worcestershire, made from specific perry-pear varieties.

POLYPHENOLS The family of compounds from West Country (and French) cider apples that provide volatile phenolic characters on the aroma and tannins in the mouth.

POMACE The dry, spent apple pulp left after pressing. Normally fed to livestock or used in an anaerobic digester to produce green electricity.

PRESS The piece of equipment that applies pressure to pulp from freshly milled apples to separate the juice from the solid component (*see* pomace).

PULP Freshly chopped apple straight out of the mill (scratter) and waiting to be pressed.

QUALITY CONTROL Normally used in inverted commas, this is a fancy term for drinking cider! It forms a crucial part of the cider maker's ability to ensure that the product meets expectations and to further develop the palate.

SCRUMPY In the UK, a rough, cloudy and acetic cider.

SORBITOL Unfermentable sugar found in pears which, if consumed in large quantities, can have a laxative effect!

SULPHIDES Chemicals producing a fault in the cider caused by stressed yeast. Hydrogen sulphide provides ammonia/eggy aromas and flavours, while the more complex disulphides are redolent of rotten cabbages and dirty drains.

SULPHITES More accurately known as sulphur dioxide, sulphites are used by most cider makers at two stages in the process: early on as an anti-microbial agent and later as a preservative.

TANNIN A type of polyphenol from West Country cider apples that provides bitterness, astringency, mouthfeel, texture and complexity.

YEAST Along with the selection of apple variety, the action of yeast has the greatest impact over the resultant flavour of a cider. Most commercial cider is made with an introduced, cultured, Champagne-type yeast. Many craft producers allow a wild fermentation to take place, increasing the chance of spoilage, but also leading to more interesting and complex ciders.

ACKNOWLEDGMENTS

Love and thanks, first and foremost, must go to my folks, Chris and Tony, who have unconditionally supported my global cider adventures. I genuinely wouldn't be doing this without them.

For sage advice, ego-checking, micky-taking, a place to stay and a fabulous distraction during hard times, I thank my brothers Alex and Laurie, my sisters-in-law Toni and Claire, my nephews Jude and Theo and my niece Lola. Love you guys.

I have been fortunate to have several influential cider mentors along my journey: Mike Johnson from Ross Cider, Jonathan Blair and Helen Thomas from Westons, and Fen Tyler. So much of what I know comes directly from them. I heartily thank them all for the opportunities they have provided and the wisdom they have imparted.

Graham and Deb Biggs and Brett Mason from The Naked Creative in Herefordshire are not only dear friends but helped me realize the dream of The Ciderologist back in 2015 and have been unwavering in their support ever since. You guys are lush.

To my friend, cider maker extraordinaire, progressive industry voice and US tour manager Tom Oliver, I say cheers for all his championing work and support, and for getting me on the train that one time in the Hudson Valley (what happens on tour, stays on tour).

To Bill Bradshaw for his cider passion, stunningly evocative storytelling of the cider world through his lens and for somehow making me not look like a complete turnip, I say cheers, mate.

To all my friends, cidery or otherwise, who have ushered me along this cider path, thank you so much. You know who you are, and there are far too many to mention here, but an especially big shout out to Ant and Dave, the Clique, Broome Crew, Norman and Annie Stanier, the Hewitts, Sophatron, Roo and Katy, Wonderful Wellingtonians (Jason, Jane and Rob), Shane Street and family, all the Moutere Massive (Trudes, Yvan, Vanessa, John, Becky, Timmy and Franzis), Rob Grey, Ellen Capewell and The Coach House Collective.

Thank you to Sarah Ford, Ellie Corbett, Juliette Norsworthy and all at Octopus for having a punt on me, and for not flipping out when I (inevitably) missed all my deadlines!

Big love to Dymock and The Shire for providing constant inspiration and wonderment.

But most importantly, thank you to the thousands of cider and perry makers all across the planet who produce these wonderful drinks. It is your passion, skill, knowledge, dedication, determination and sense of fun that drives me to tell this awesome story. Please, for the love of Pomona, don't stop what you're doing. Cider's time is about to come. For real.

Wassail!

PICTURE CREDITS